555 QUESTIONS AND ANSWERS
ABOUT PEOPLE, PLACES, AND PLANET EARTH

QUESTIONS
& ANSWERS

Bath · New York · Singapore · Hong Kong · Cologne · Delhi · Melbourne

This edition published by Parragon in 2009

Parragon
Queen Street House
4 Queen Street
Bath BA1 1HE, UK

Copyright © Parragon Books Ltd 2003, 2009

Written by: John Farndon, Ian James, Jinny Johnson, Fiona Macdonald,
Claudia Martin, Angela Royston, Philip Steele, and Martin Walters

Consultants: Sarah Durant, Philip Parker, John Williams, and Astrid Wingler

This edition produced by Tall Tree Ltd, London

Americanizer: Michael Janes
Proofreader: Joanne Brooks

ISBN 978-1-4075-1314-0

Printed in China

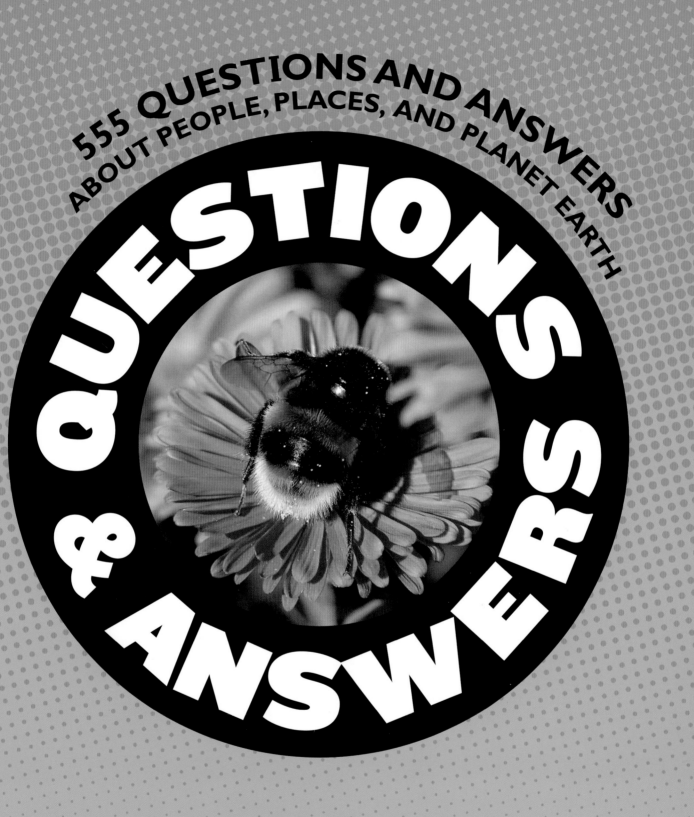

QUESTIONS & ANSWERS

555 QUESTIONS AND ANSWERS
ABOUT PEOPLE, PLACES, AND PLANET EARTH

PaRragon

Bath · New York · Singapore · Hong Kong · Cologne · Delhi · Melbourne

Contents

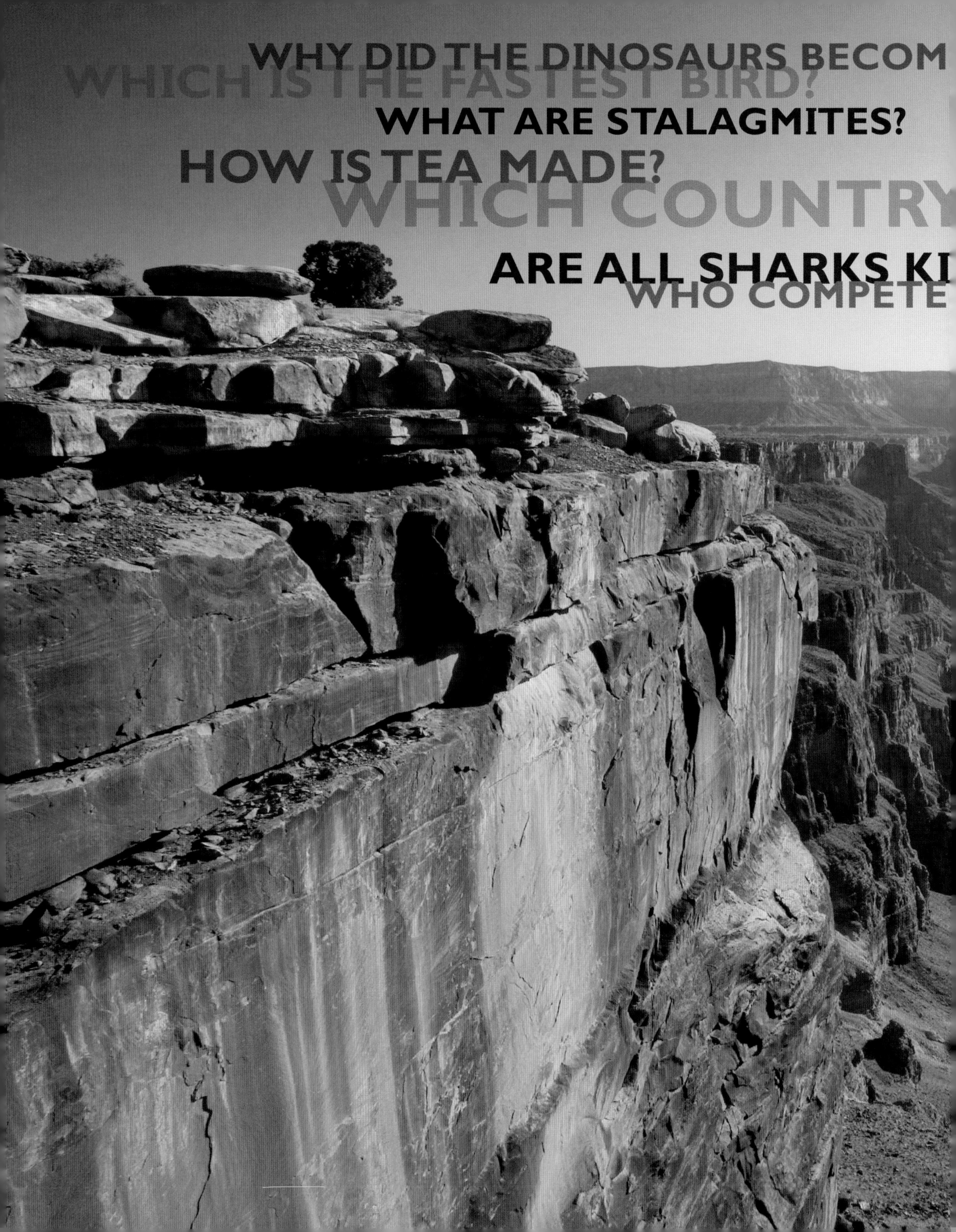

WHICH IS THE FASTEST BIRD?

WHY DID THE DINOSAURS BECOM

WHAT ARE STALAGMITES?

HOW IS TEA MADE?

WHICH COUNTRY

ARE ALL SHARKS KI

WHO COMPETE

XTINCT?

CAN HIPPOS SWIM?

WHAT IS DIWALI?

WHAT IS THE LARGEST FLOWER?

WHERE DO DRUMS TALK?

FITS INSIDE A CITY?

CAN DESERTS BE FARMED?

ERS?

N THE SPACE RACE?

WHO WERE THE INCAS?

WHAT IS A POW-WOW?

Introduction

Do you know where soldiers wear skirts? Or where you can catch a train into the sky? Have you ever wanted to find out how the Egyptians made mummies? Or what makes a volcano erupt? Which is the most deadly snake? And which whale can sing? In this book, you will find the answers to 555 fascinating questions you've always wanted to ask— covering everything from fossils to e-mails, from earthquakes to skyscrapers, from life-saving plants to murderous Vikings, from eating spiders to wearing clogs.

History

Ancient Egypt >

The ancient Egyptian civilization grew up along the Nile River, in northeastern Africa, from about 3150 BC. Under the rule of kings known as pharaohs, the Egyptians made great strides in building, art, and science.

> HOW OLD ARE THE PYRAMIDS?

The first pyramid was built between 2630 and 2611 BC. It had stepped sides and was built for King Djoser. Before then, pharaohs were buried in flat-top mounds called mastabas. The last pyramid in Egypt itself was built around 1530 BC.

> WHY WERE THE PYRAMIDS BUILT?

The pyramids are huge tombs for pharaohs and nobility. The Egyptians believed that dead people's spirits could live on after death if their bodies were carefully preserved. It was especially important to preserve the bodies of dead pharaohs because their spirits would help the kingdom of Egypt to survive. So they made dead bodies into mummies, and buried them in these splendid tombs along with clothes and jewels.

PYRAMID OF KHAFRE

Pharaoh Khafre's pyramid was completed in about 2530 BC in Giza, near Cairo.

▸ HOW WAS A PYRAMID BUILT?

By manpower! Thousands of laborers worked in the hot sun to clear the site, lay the foundations, drag building stone from the quarry, and lift it into place. Most of the laborers were ordinary farmers, who worked as builders to pay their dues to the pharaoh. Expert craftsmen cut the stone into blocks and fitted them together.

▸ WHY DID EGYPTIANS TREASURE SCARABS?

Scarabs (beetles) collect animal dung and roll it into little balls. To the Egyptians, these dung balls looked like the life-giving sun, so they hoped that scarabs would bring them long life.

▸ HOW WERE CORPSES MUMMIFIED?

Making a mummy was a complicated and expensive process. First, most of the soft internal organs were removed, then the body was packed in chemicals and left to dry out. Finally, it was wrapped in resin-soaked linen bandages, and placed in a beautifully decorated coffin.

WHY WAS THE NILE RIVER SO IMPORTANT?

Because Egypt got almost no rain. But every year the Nile flooded the fields along its banks, bringing fresh water and rich black silt, which helped crops to grow. Farmers dug irrigation channels to carry water to distant fields. All of Egypt's great cities lay on the river, which was also a vital thoroughfare for boats carrying people and goods.

FELUCCA

Wooden boats called feluccas have sailed on the Nile for millennia.

MUMMY

After embalming, a body was wrapped in a sheet and placed in a coffin to keep it safe.

Ancient Greece and Rome >

Starting from the eighth century BC, a great civilization began to grow in Greece, allowing architects, thinkers, and artists to thrive. But by the third century BC, a new power was taking over in the region—the Romans.

> WHY DID THE ROMAN EMPEROR HADRIAN BUILD A WALL?

To help guard the frontiers of the Roman Empire, which then spread from Britain to North Africa. The wall ran from coast to coast across the north of Britain. Emperor Hadrian (ruled AD 117–138) made many visits to frontier provinces to encourage the Roman troops stationed there.

WHY DID GREEK TEMPLES HAVE SO MANY COLUMNS?

The style may have been copied from ancient Greek palaces, which had lots of wooden pillars to hold up the roof.

GREEK TEMPLE

Greek architecture was based on balance and order.

HADRIAN'S WALL

Roman soldiers were based along the wall, looking out for raiders from the lands beyond.

❯ WHY DID THE GREEKS BUILD SO MANY TEMPLES?

Because they worshipped so many different goddesses and gods! The Greeks believed each god needed a home where their spirit could live. And every god had special powers, which visitors to the temple prayed for. Zeus was the god of the sky and Aphrodite was the goddess of love.

❯ WHAT WERE THE ORIGINAL OLYMPIC GAMES?

The Greeks set up an athletic competition in the city of Olympia in 776 BC. It was held every four years, with athletes traveling from all over Greece to compete at events, including running, boxing, and wrestling.

❯ WHO WERE ROMAN CENTURIONS?

Centurions were army officers. They dressed for parade in a decorated metal breastplate and a helmet topped with a crest of horsehair. They also wore shin guards, called greaves.

❯ DID THE ROMANS HAVE CENTRAL HEATING?

Yes. They invented a system called the "hypocaust." Hot air, heated by a wood-burning furnace, was circulated through pipes underneath the floor.

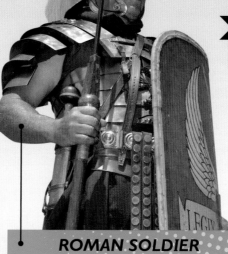

ROMAN SOLDIER

This reconstruction of a soldier's dress shows his armor, spear, and sword.

Vikings >

The Vikings came from Norway, Denmark, and Sweden. Starting from around AD 800 until AD 1100, these warriors made raids across Europe, killing, burning, and carrying away all that they could manage.

> WERE THE VIKINGS GOOD SAILORS?

Yes. They sailed for thousands of miles across the icy northern oceans in open wooden boats, known as longboats. They learned how to navigate by observing the sun and the stars.

LONGBOAT •————————————

A reconstruction of a Viking longboat shows the streamlined, lightweight design.

> WHAT GODS DID THE VIKINGS BELIEVE IN?

The Vikings prayed to many different gods. Thor sent thunder and protected craftsmen. Odin was the god of wisdom and war. Kindly goddess Freya gave peace and fruitful crops.

> WHAT WERE VIKING SHIPS MADE OF?

Narrow, flexible strips of wood, attached to a solid wooden backbone called a keel. Viking warships were long and narrow, and could sail very fast. They were powered by men rowing, or by the wind trapped in big square sails.

➤ DID THE VIKINGS REACH NORTH AMERICA?

Yes, around AD 1000. A bold adventurer named Leif Ericsson sailed westward from Greenland until he reached "Vinland" (present-day Newfoundland, Canada). He built a farmstead there, but quarreled with the local people, and decided to return home.

LEIF ERICSSON

This adventurer was based in a Viking colony in Greenland.

➤ WHAT DOES "VIKING" MEAN?

The word "Viking" comes from the old Scandinavian word *vik*, which means "a narrow bay by the sea." That's where the Vikings lived. It was hard to make a living in the cold Viking homelands, so Viking men raided wealthier lands. But not all Vikings were raiders. Some traveled to new places to settle, and many were hunters and farmers who never left home.

WHAT DID VIKINGS SEIZE ON THEIR RAIDS?

All kinds of treasure. A hoard of silver (below), including coins and belt buckles, was buried by Vikings in the tenth century and discovered by workmen in Lancashire, England, in 1840. The Vikings also kidnapped people to sell as slaves.

Aztecs, Maya, and Incas >

Before the Spanish conquest of the Americas in the sixteenth century, Central and South America were home to some of the world's greatest civilizations. Beautiful cities and pyramids were built, while scholars studied astronomy and mathematics.

> ## WHO WERE THE INCAS?

A people who lived in the Andes Mountains of South America (part of present-day Peru and Ecuador). They ruled a mighty empire from the early fifteenth century to early sixteenth century AD.

MACHU PICCHU

This Inca city was built of polished stone around AD 1460.

➤ WHO BUILT PYRAMIDS TO STUDY THE STARS?

Priests of the Maya civilization, which was powerful in Central America between AD 200 and 900. They built huge, stepped pyramids, with temples and observatories at the top. The Maya were expert astronomers and mathematicians, and worked out very accurate calendars.

➤ WHO WERE THE AZTECS?

The Aztecs were wandering hunters who arrived in Mexico about AD 1200. They fought against the people already living there, built a city called Tenochtitlán on an island in a marshy lake, and soon grew rich and strong.

CHICHEN ITZA

The step pyramid is topped by a temple dedicated to the Maya serpent god Kukulkan.

➤ WHO WROTE IN PICTURES?

Maya and Aztec scribes. The Maya used a system of picture symbols called glyphs. Maya and Aztecs both wrote in stitched books, called codices, using paper made from the bark of a fig tree.

➤ HOW DID THE MAYA, AZTECS, AND INCAS LOSE THEIR POWER?

They were conquered by soldiers from Spain, who arrived in the Americas in the early sixteenth century, looking for treasure, especially gold.

TOP QUESTION ?

WHY WERE LLAMAS SO IMPORTANT?

Because they could survive in the Incas' mountain homeland, over 10,000 feet above sea level. It is cold and windy there, and few plants grow. The Incas wove cloth from llama wool, and used llamas to carry loads up steep mountain paths.

The Islamic world →

Between about AD 700 and 1200, the Islamic world experienced a period of great power. It led the rest of the globe in learning, invention, and architecture. Islamic leaders controlled lands from southern Spain to northwest India.

› WHAT IS ISLAM?

The religious faith taught by the Prophet Muhammad. People who follow the faith of Islam are called Muslims. Muhammad was a religious leader who lived in Arabia from AD 570 to 632. He taught people to worship Allah, the one God. At its peak, the vast Islamic World—stretching from Spain and North Africa, through Central Asia to northwest India—was ruled by Muslim princes and governed by Islamic laws.

› WHO WERE THE MONGOLS?

They were nomads who roamed across Central Asia. In AD 1206, the Mongol tribes united under a leader known as Genghis Khan ("Supreme Ruler") and set out to conquer the world. At its peak, the Mongol Empire spread from China to eastern Europe.

LA MEZQUITA

The Muslim rulers of Spain built a great mosque in the city of Córdoba starting from AD 784.

> WHO INVENTED THE ASTROLABE?

The astrolabe was perfected by Muslim scientists who lived and worked in the Middle East in the eighth century. Astrolabes were scientific instruments that helped sailors find their position when they were at sea. They worked by measuring the height of the sun above the horizon.

> WHO LIVED IN A CIRCULAR CITY?

The citizens of Baghdad, which was founded in AD 762 by the caliph (ruler) al-Mansur. He employed builders and architects to create a huge circular city, surrounded by strong walls. There were palaces, government offices, mosques, hospitals, schools, libraries, and gardens.

ASTROLABE

Astrolabes can be used for navigation and timekeeping.

> WHAT WERE SHIPS OF THE DESERT?

Camels owned by merchants who lived in Arabia. They were the only animals that could survive long enough without food and water to make journeys across the desert, laden with goods to sell. They stored enough nourishment in their humps to last several days.

TOP **?** QUESTION

WHAT WERE THE CRUSADES?

A series of wars fought between Christian and Muslim soldiers for control of the area around Jerusalem (in present-day Israel), which was holy to Muslims, Christians, and Jews. The Crusades began in 1095, when a Christian army attacked (right). Their main period ended in 1291, when Muslim soldiers forced the Christians to leave.

China and Japan

China was one of the earliest centers of human civilization, with its first cities founded more than 4,000 years ago. On the islands of Japan, people were making decorated pottery an amazing 12,000 years ago. Pottery found there is among the oldest in the world.

WHAT MADE CHINA SO RICH?

The inventions of Chinese farmers and engineers made the land productive. In the Middle Ages, the Chinese made spectacular strides in agriculture. They dug networks of irrigation channels to bring water to the rice fields. They built machines, such as a foot-powered pump to lift water to the fields. The emperor and government officials also ruled China very effectively, allowing it to grow wealthy.

HOW DID CHINA GET ITS NAME?

From the Qin (pronounced "chin") dynasty, the first dynasty to rule over a united China. Founded by Ch'in Shih Huang Ti, China's first emperor, it lasted from 221 to 206 BC. It was responsible for the standardization of Chinese script, weights and measures, and the contruction of the Great Wall.

GOLDEN TEMPLE

The temple was built in the fourteenth century in Kyoto, Japan.

WHERE WAS THE MIDDLE KINGDOM?

The Chinese believed their country was at the center of the world, so they called it the Middle Kingdom. In fact, for centuries, China was one of the most advanced civilizations on earth. Under the Tang and Song dynasties (AD 618–1279) Chinese cities, such as Chang'an (modern Xi'an), were the world's biggest.

FORBIDDEN CITY

Built from 1406, the palace, "forbidden" to outsiders, was home to China's emperors.

INNER COURT

A walkway leads to the Palace of Heavenly Purity, where the emperor received guests.

WHO VALUED HONOR MORE THAN LIFE?

Japanese warriors, called samurai, who were powerful starting from around the twelfth century. They were taught to fight according to a strict code of honor. They believed that it was better to commit suicide than to face defeat.

WHICH RULERS CLAIMED DESCENT FROM THE SUN GODDESS?

The emperors of Japan. The first Japanese emperor lived around 660 BC. His descendants ruled until AD 1192. After that, shoguns (army generals) ran the government, leaving the emperors with only religious and ceremonial powers.

WHAT WAS CHINA'S BEST-KEPT SECRET?

How to make silk. For centuries, no one else knew how. Chinese women fed silk-moth grubs on mulberry leaves, and the grubs spun thread and wrapped themselves in it to make cocoons. Workers steamed the cocoons to kill the grubs, unwound the thread, dyed it, and wove it into cloth.

SILKWORM

Silkworms have been kept in China for at least 5,000 years.

Europe >

After the Roman Empire released its hold on the rest of Europe, the countries of Europe were ruled by kings, queens, and nobles. As they farmed the land, many ordinary people lived in great poverty.

WHEN WERE THE MIDDLE AGES?

When historians refer to the Middle Ages, or the medieval period, they usually mean the time from the collapse of the Roman Empire, around AD 500, to about AD 1500.

WHO FARMED LAND THEY DID NOT OWN?

Poor peasant families. Under medieval law, all the land belonged to the king, or to rich nobles. The peasants lived in little cottages in return for rent or for work on the land. Sometimes the peasants protested or tried to run away.

WHO DID BATTLE IN METAL SUITS?

Kings, lords, and knights who lived in Europe during the Middle Ages. In those days, men from aristocratic families were brought up to fight and lead soldiers into battle. It was their duty, according to law. From around AD 1000, knights wore simple chain-mail tunics, but by about 1450, armor was made of shaped metal plates, carefully pieced together. The most expensive suits of armor were decorated with engraved patterns or polished gold.

ARMOR

Medieval armor covered the body from head to toe.

TOP QUESTION ?

WHO BUILT CASTLES AND CATHEDRALS?

Kings, queens, and nobles. The first castles were wooden forts. Later, they were built of stone. Cathedrals were very big churches in cities or towns. They were built to reflect God's glory and to bring honor to those who had paid for them.

WHO WAS THE VIRGIN QUEEN?

Elizabeth I of England (above), who reigned from 1558 to 1603, at a time when many people believed that women were too weak to rule. Elizabeth proved them wrong. Under her leadership, England grew stronger. She never married and ruled alone.

NOTRE DAME

The Bishop of Paris ordered the construction of the cathedral in 1163.

WHICH RUSSIAN CZAR WAS TERRIBLE?

Ivan IV, who was known as Ivan the Terrible. He became czar, or emperor, in 1533, when he was three years old. He was clever but ruthless, and killed everyone who opposed him. He passed laws removing many of the rights of peasants, making them almost serfs, like slaves.

Africa and India >

By the Middle Ages, African cities were rich centers of learning and trade, with merchants traveling as far afield as India and Southeast Asia. And throughout its long history, India has been home to many great empires, from the Mauryans (322–185 BC) to the Mughals.

WHERE DID DHOWS SAIL TO TRADE?

Dhows were ships built for rich merchants living in trading ports, such as Kilwa, in East Africa. They sailed to the Red Sea and the Persian Gulf to buy pearls and perfumes, across the Indian Ocean to India to buy silks and jewels, and to Malaysia and Indonesia to buy spices.

WHICH AFRICAN CITY HAD A FAMOUS UNIVERSITY?

Timbuktu, in present-day Mali, West Africa. The city was founded in the eleventh century and became a great center of learning for Muslim scholars from many lands. Timbuktu also had several mosques and markets, a royal palace, and a library.

DHOW
A traditional wooden dhow is powered by triangular-shaped sails.

WHICH KINGS BUILT TALL TOWERS?

Shona kings of southeast Africa, who built a city called Great Zimbabwe. Zimbabwe means "stone houses." The city was also a massive fortress. From inside this fortress, the Shona kings ruled a rich empire from AD 1100 to 1600.

➤ WHO FOUNDED A NEW RELIGION IN INDIA?

Guru Nanak, a religious teacher who lived in northwest India from 1469 to 1539. He taught that there is one God, and that people should respect one another equally, as brothers and sisters. His followers became known as Sikhs.

➤ HOW LONG DID THE MUGHALS RULE INDIA?

For more than three centuries, starting from 1526 until 1858. The Mughal dynasty was descended from the great Mongol warrior Genghis Khan (Mughal is a north Indian way of writing Mongol). The last Mughal emperor was toppled when the British government took control of India.

GOLDEN TEMPLE OF AMRITSAR

The beautiful temple, begun in 1574, is one of the most important places of worship for Sikhs.

TAJ MAHAL

To construct the building, 20,000 workers were recruited from as far afield as Persia and Syria.

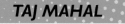

➤ WHO BUILT THE TAJ MAHAL?

The Mughal emperor Shah Jehan (ruled 1628–58). He was so sad when his wife Mumtaz Mahal died that he built a lovely tomb for her, called the Taj Mahal. It is made of pure white marble decorated with gold and semiprecious stones.

Pacific Ocean lands >

Australia, New Zealand, and the Polynesian islands lie in the Pacific Ocean. They were probably first colonized by voyagers from Southeast Asia. From the sixteenth century, Europeans started to explore the Pacific lands.

> WHO WAS THE FIRST TO SAIL AROUND THE WORLD?

It was sailors in the ship *Victoria*, owned by Ferdinand Magellan, a Portuguese explorer. In 1519, he sailed westward from Europe, but was killed fighting in the Philippines. His captain, Sebastian Elcano, managed to complete the voyage, and returned home to Europe, weak but triumphant, in 1522.

TOP ? QUESTION

HOW DID SAILORS HELP SCIENCE?

European sailors often observed the plants, fish, and animals as they traveled, and brought specimens home with them. When Captain James Cook explored the Pacific Ocean, he took artists and scientists with him to record what they saw.

CAPTAIN COOK

This drawing was made by Captain Cook's official artist, John Webber, when the expedition arrived in Hawaii in 1799.

> DID THE ABORIGINALS ALWAYS LIVE IN AUSTRALIA?

No, they probably arrived from Southeast Asia about 60,000 years ago, when the sea around Australia was shallower than today. They may have traveled by land or in small boats. It is believed that the Aboriginal settlers introduced dogs to Australia—the ancestors of today's dingoes. They were used as guard and hunting dogs, and to keep Aboriginal people warm as they slept around campfires in the desert, which is cold at night.

➤ WHO WERE THE FIRST PEOPLE TO DISCOVER NEW ZEALAND?

The Maoris. They began a mass migration from other Pacific Islands at around AD 1150, but remains dating back to AD 800 have been found in New Zealand.

MAORI CARVING

Wood carving—on buildings and decorative items—is an important part of traditional Maori culture.

➤ HOW DID THE POLYNESIAN PEOPLE CROSS THE PACIFIC OCEAN?

By sailing and paddling big outrigger canoes. They steered by studying the waves and the stars, and made maps out of twigs and shells to help themselves navigate.

POLYNESIAN CANOE

The canoe has an outrigger, or support, on one side for stability.

North America ⟩

The earliest evidence for the settlement of North America dates from 14,000 years ago. These ancestors of today's Native Americans were farmers, hunters, and traders. The first Europeans to settle in North America arrived in the mid-sixteenth century.

⟩ WHAT STORIES DO TOTEM POLES TELL?

Native American people who lived in the forests of northwest North America carved tall totem poles to record their family's history, and to retell ancient legends about the powerful spirits that lived in all rocks, mountains, wild animals, and trees.

⟩ WHO LIVED IN TENTS ON THE GREAT PLAINS?

Native American hunters, such as the Sioux and the Cheyenne. After Europeans settled in North America, bringing horses with them, Native Americans spent summer on the grasslands of the Great Plains, following herds of buffalo, which they killed for meat and skins. In winter, they camped in sheltered valleys. Before the Europeans brought horses, Native Americans were mainly farmers.

TOTEM POLE

The word "totem" comes from the Ojibwe people of Canada's word for family or tribe.

⟩ WHY DID THE PILGRIMS LEAVE HOME?

The Pilgrims were a group of English families with strong religious beliefs, who quarreled with Church leaders and the government. In 1620, they sailed in the *Mayflower* to North America, to build a new community where they could practice their religion in peace.

❯ WHEN DID THE USA BECOME INDEPENDENT?

On July 4, 1776, 13 English colonies (where most Europeans in North America had settled) made a Declaration of Independence, refusing to be ruled by Britain any longer. They became a new nation, the United States of America. Britain sent more troops to win the colonies back, but was defeated in 1783.

❯ WHO WERE THE FIRST EUROPEANS TO SETTLE IN NORTH AMERICA?

Spanish colonists, who settled in present-day Florida and California, beginning around 1540. An English settlement began in Jamestown, Virginia, in 1607 and in Massachusetts in 1620.

LIBERTY BELL

According to tradition, the bell was rung to announce the Declaration of Independence in 1776.

TOP ? QUESTION

WHY DID A CIVIL WAR BREAK OUT?

The Civil War (1861–65), between the northern and southern states, was caused mainly by a quarrel over slavery. The southern states relied on African slaves working in their cotton plantations. The northern states wanted slavery banned. After four years, the northern states won, and slavery was abolished.

The Industrial Revolution >

The Industrial Revolution was a huge change in the way people worked and goods were produced. Machines in large factories replaced craftspeople working by hand. It began around 1775 in Britain and spread slowly to the United States and other countries in Europe.

FACTORY WORK

Workers took long shifts among dangerous machines.

> WHEN DID THE FIRST TRAINS RUN?

Horse-drawn railroad wagons had been used to haul coal and stone from mines and quarries since the sixteenth century, but the first passenger railroad was opened by George Stephenson in the north of England in 1825. Its locomotives were powered by steam.

> WHO WORKED IN THE FIRST FACTORIES?

Thousands of poor men and women moved from the countryside to live in fast-growing factory towns. They hoped to find regular work and more pay. Wages in factories were better than those on farms, but factories were often dirty and dangerous.

STEPHENSON'S ROCKET

In 1829, George Stephenson built a groundbreaking steam locomotive, called the *Rocket*.

> ## DID CHILDREN LEAD BETTER LIVES THEN?

No. Many worked 16 hours a day in factories and mines. Large numbers were killed in accidents with machinery, or died from breathing coal dust or chemical fumes. After 1802, governments began to pass laws to protect child workers.

> ## WHY WERE DRAINS AND TOILETS SO IMPORTANT?

Because without them, diseases carried in sewage could spread quickly in crowded industrial towns. Pottery making was one of the first mass-production industries—and the factories made thousands of toilets!

> ## HOW DID THE RAILROADS CHANGE PEOPLE'S LIVES?

They helped trade and industry to grow by carrying raw materials to factories, and finished goods from factories to stores. They carried fresh foods from farms to cities. They made it easier for people to travel and encouraged a whole new vacation industry.

WHY WAS STEAM POWER SO IMPORTANT?

The development of the steam engine was one of the key breakthroughs that allowed the Industrial Revolution to take place. A steam engine can do work—such as powering machines or trains—using hot steam. Steam power allowed quicker production of goods in factories (below) and then their swift transportation to buyers.

The Modern Age →

Since 1900, the world has changed in many ways. Women now play an important part in government. Technology has revolutionized our lives. But wars and poverty still blight the world.

WAR GRAVES

Around 10 million soldiers died in World War 1.

> ## WHAT WAS THE LONG MARCH?

A grueling march across China, covering 5,000 miles, made by around 100,000 Communists escaping their enemies. They were led by Mao Tse-tung, who became ruler of China in 1949.

> ## WHO FOUGHT AND DIED IN THE TRENCHES?

Millions of young men during World War I (1914–18). Trenches were ditches dug into the ground. They were meant to shelter soldiers from gunfire, but offered little protection from shells exploding overhead. Soon, the trenches filled up with mud, water, rats, and dead bodies.

TOP QUESTION ?

WHO DROPPED THE FIRST ATOMIC BOMB?

On August 6, 1945, the United States bombed Hiroshima in Japan, killing 66,000 people instantly. Two-thirds of the city's buildings were destroyed (right). Days later, Japan surrendered, ending World War II.

➤ WHAT WAS THE COLD WAR?

A time of dangerous tension from the 1940s to the 1980s between the United States and the USSR, the two strongest nations in the world. The United States believed in democracy and capitalism; the USSR was Communist—and the countries distrusted one another. The superpowers never fought face to face, but their enmity drew them into local conflicts around the globe.

MAN ON THE MOON

The American astronaut Buzz Aldrin (left) was the second man to set foot on the Moon. The first man on the Moon was his companion Neil Armstrong, who took this famous photo.

➤ WHO TOOK PART IN THE SPACE RACE?

The USSR and the United States. Each tried to rival the other's achievements in space. The USSR took the lead by launching the first satellite in 1957, but the Americans won the race by landing the first man on the Moon in 1969.

Countries of the world

A Crowded World

All human beings are basically the same, wherever they live. We may speak different languages and have different ideas. Our parents may give us dark or pale skin, blue eyes or brown. But in the end we are all members of the same family, living on our increasingly crowded earth.

WHO ARE THE WORLD'S PEOPLES?

Human beings who share the same history or language make up "a people," or "ethnic group." Sometimes many different peoples share a country. More than 120 peoples live in Tanzania, Africa.

WHICH COUNTRY HAS THE MOST PEOPLE?

More people live in China than anywhere else in the world. They number about 1,320,000,000 and most live in the big cities of the east and the south. In the far west of China, there are empty deserts and lonely mountains.

HOW MANY PEOPLE LIVE IN THE WORLD?

Billions! In 2008, there were about 6.7 billion human beings living on our planet. That's more than twice as many as 50 years ago.

WHERE ARE THE MOST CROWDED PLACES IN THE WORLD?

Tiny countries and large cities may house millions of people. Bangladesh is one of the most crowded places in the world. There are more than 2,000 people per square mile.

NEW YORK

In busy cities where land is scarce, people have built tall skyscrapers.

> IS THERE ENOUGH ROOM FOR EVERYBODY?

Every minute, about 260 babies are born around the world. Imagine how they would cry if they were all put together! By the year 2050, there will probably be 9.3 billion people in the world. If the planet's population were to continue to grow at the same rate for much longer, sooner or later the world would be just too crowded. Perhaps, some time in the future, people may have to live in towns under the ocean or even on other planets, where they would need a special supply of air in order to stay alive.

The World's population

Some parts of the world are rich in natural resources, such as good soil for growing crops, or oil that can be used for powering machinery. Such resources make countries wealthy. Elsewhere, people may live in poverty and be forced to migrate in search of work and food.

HAVE PEOPLE ALWAYS LIVED WHERE THEY LIVE NOW?

During history, many peoples have moved huge distances, or migrated. The Polynesians may have taken 2,500 years to cross the Pacific Ocean and settle its islands. In modern times, many people have traveled to the United States in search of better lives.

AFRICAN LAND

Many parts of Africa have poor soil and lack rain.

> HAVE HUMANS CHANGED OUR PLANET?

Over the ages, humans have changed the face of the world we live in. They have chopped down forests and dammed rivers. They have built big cities and roads.

> WHY ARE SOME LANDS RICHER THAN OTHERS?

Some lands have good soil, where crops can grow. Some have oil, which is worth a lot of money. But other countries have poor soil, little rain, and no minerals. However hard people work there, they struggle to survive.

❯ WHERE DO PEOPLE LIVE?

Humans live wherever they can find food and water, which they need to stay alive. Nobody at all lives in Antarctica, the icy southern wilderness. Scientists do visit bases there, so that they can study rocks, icebergs, and penguins. The Sahara in Africa is a land of burning-hot sand and rocks. It has just a few places, called oases, where people can get the water they need to survive.

❯ WHAT IS A CONTINENT?

The big masses of land that make up the earth's surface are called continents. The biggest continent of all is Asia, which is home to more than 3.9 billion people.

IMMIGRANTS

In the twentieth century, 46 million immigrants arrived in the United States.

❯ WHICH IS THE WORLD'S RICHEST COUNTRY?

Some economists say that Qatar, in the Middle East, is the richest country because it exports huge amounts of oil and gas, which are used as fuel.

RIO DE JANEIRO

Many people in Rio, in Brazil, live in packed shanty towns called *favelas*.

Countries and flags ❯

There are more than 200 countries in the world. Some of these nations rule themselves, while some are ruled by other countries. The number of countries constantly changes as some join together to make a single nation, while others break up into smaller states.

❯ WHAT IS A COUNTRY?

A country is an area of land under the rule of a single government. Its borders have to be agreed with neighboring countries, although this sometimes leads to arguments. Countries that rule themselves are called independent. Countries that are ruled by other countries are called dependencies.

❯ DO ALL PEOPLES HAVE A COUNTRY THEY CAN CALL THEIR OWN?

No, the ancient homelands of some peoples are divided up between other countries. The lands of the Kurdish people are split between several nations.

❯ WHERE CAN YOU SEE ALL THE FLAGS OF THE UNITED NATIONS?

Rows of flags fly outside the headquarters of the United Nations in New York City. Most of the world's countries belong to this organization, which tries to solve all kinds of problems around the globe.

> WHICH COUNTRY FITS INSIDE A CITY?

The world's smallest nation is an area within the city of Rome, in Italy. It is called Vatican City and is the headquarters of the Roman Catholic Church. Fewer than 1,000 people live there.

VATICAN CITY

The Pope is the head of government of Vatican City, which is about 0.17 square miles.

> WHY DO COUNTRIES HAVE FLAGS?

Flags show bold patterns and bright colors. Many flags are symbols of a nation, or of its regions. The designs on flags often tell us about a country or its history. The flag of Kenya includes a traditional shield and spears, while the flag of Lebanon includes a cedar tree—cedar trees were plentiful there in ancient times.

> WHICH IS THE OLDEST NATIONAL FLAG?

The oldest flag still in use is Denmark's. It is a white cross on a red background and was first used in the fourteenth century. It is called the Dannebrog, meaning "Danish cloth."

UNITED NATIONS

Today, 192 countries belong to the United Nations. The organization's own flag is blue.

The world's countries range from tiny independent island nations to vast countries made up of numerous states or provinces. Some nations are ruled by countries that lie on the other side of the world, such as the British Virgin Islands in the Caribbean Sea.

CANADIAN QUEEN

Canada was once part of the British Empire. Today, it is independent, but Great Britain's Queen Elizabeth II is still on banknotes as the state's figurehead.

› WHAT IS AN EMPIRE?

An empire is a country that rules over many other countries and nations. The British Empire was the world's largest empire. In 1922, it covered over one-quarter of the world's land.

RUSSIAN LANDS

Russia shares land borders with 14 other countries, from Norway in the west to China in the east. It covers all of northern Asia and takes up 40 percent of Europe.

› HOW MANY INDEPENDENT COUNTRIES ARE THERE?

Currently, there are more than 190 independent countries in the world—the number changes from one year to the next.

› WHICH IS THE BIGGEST COUNTRY IN THE WORLD?

The gigantic Russian Federation takes up almost 7 million square miles of the earth's surface. It spreads into two continents, Europe and Asia, and its clocks are set at 11 different times.

WHAT ARE COUNTIES AND STATES?

If you look at the map of a country, you will see that it is divided up into smaller regions. These often have their own local laws and are known as states, provinces, counties, or departments.

❯ HOW MANY DEPENDENCIES ARE THERE IN THE WORLD?

Around 38 of the world's nations are still ruled by other countries. They include many tiny islands in the Caribbean Sea—such as Montserrat and the Cayman Islands, which are governed by Great Britain—and in the Atlantic and Pacific oceans.

UNITED STATES

The United States of America is composed of 50 states.

The countries of the world are governed in many different ways. In a democracy, people vote for a political party to make the decisions. In some countries, people do not have the right to vote freely and are ruled over by a dictator.

HOW DO YOU RECOGNIZE KINGS AND QUEENS?

For ceremonies kings and queens wear traditional robes, and some wear crowns and carry symbols of royal power, such as golden scepters. The traditional rulers of the Yoruba people of Nigeria wear a beaded crown.

HOW DOES ANYONE GET TO BE A KING OR QUEEN?

Normally you have to be a prince or princess, born into a royal family. In the past, kings and queens were powerful. Today, their role is more as the nation's figurehead. They visit hospitals and meet other heads of state as representatives of their country.

TOP QUESTION ?

WHAT IS A REPUBLIC?

It's a country that has no king or queen. France is a republic. Over 200 years ago, the French king had his head chopped off during a revolution. The United States of America was ruled by the British king until it fought the Revolutionary War (1775–83).

REVOLUTIONARY WAR

British troops in the American Revolutionary War wore red coats.

CROWN JEWELS

The British Crown Jewels include all the crowns owned by the royal family.

WHAT IS A GOVERNMENT?

The members of the government run the country. They pass new laws on everything from schools to hospitals and businesses. Countries where the people can choose their government by voting for a political party are called democracies. Some countries are ruled by dictators. These countries do not hold free elections or have a choice of political parties.

WHAT IS A HEAD OF STATE?

The most important person in a country is the head of state. This may be a king or a queen or an elected president. The head of state takes part in ceremonies and often rides in a big car with a flag on it.

WHICH IS THE WORLD'S OLDEST ROYAL FAMILY?

The Japanese royal family has produced a long line of 125 reigning emperors over a period of thousands of years.

JAPANESE ROYALTY

Emperor Akihito reads from a scroll during a ceremony to make him Emperor of Japan in 1990.

Elections and laws >

Every country has laws. These are a system of rules that govern everything from how we elect our leaders to how we should behave toward each other. Laws are created by governments, while judges and courts decide what should happen when laws are broken.

> WHO RULES THE BIRDS?

Traditionally, the king or queen of England owns all the swans on the River Thames, except for those marked in a special ceremony that takes place each summer.

> WHAT ARE "JANA-GANA-MANA" AND "GOD SAVE THE QUEEN"?

Both of them are national anthems or songs. The first tune is played to show respect to India, the second to the United Kingdom. National anthems are played at important occasions, such as the Olympic Games.

➤ WHERE DO JUDGES WEAR BIG WIGS?

In Great Britain, judges wear old-fashion wigs. This is meant to show that the judge is not in court as a private person but as someone who stands for the law of the land.

➤ WHERE IS THE BIGGEST GENERAL ELECTION?

More than 670 million people are eligible to vote in general elections in India. They can cast their votes at one of more than a million electronic voting machines around the country.

ENGLISH JUDGES

The wigs worn by judges are in the style fashionable in eighteenth-century London.

➤ WHICH IS THE WORLD'S OLDEST PARLIAMENT?

A parliament is a meeting place where new laws are discussed and approved. The oldest parliament is in Iceland. Called the Althing, it was started by Viking settlers in AD 930.

PERICLES OF ATHENS

Pericles, who lived in the fifth century BC, passed laws allowing poorer people to take part in democracy.

TOP ? QUESTION

WHO INVENTED DEMOCRACY?

The people of ancient Athens, in Greece, started the first democratic assembly nearly 2,500 years ago. It wasn't completely fair, because women and slaves weren't given the right to vote.

Language >

Around 6,900 languages are spoken in the world. The language spoken by the most people is Mandarin Chinese, which is used daily by around a billion people. English is the most widespread language. The 470 million English speakers are dotted through every single country.

> WHAT'S IN A NAME?

In Norway, there's a village called Å. In New Zealand, there's a place called Taumatawhakatangihan-gakoauauotamateaturipukaka-pikim-aungahoronukupokaiwhe-nuaki-tanatahu.

> DO WE USE DIFFERENT WAYS OF WRITING?

Many different kinds of writing have grown up around the world, using all kinds of lines and pictures. This book is printed in the Roman alphabet, which has 26 letters and is used for many languages. Chinese writers normally use about 4,000 different symbols, or characters.

CHINESE HANZI

Chinese characters, called *hanzi*, make single syllables, such as "han" and "zi."

❯ DOES EVERYBODY IN ONE COUNTRY SPEAK THE SAME LANGUAGE?

Not often. For example, families from all over the world have made their homes in the United States. In the city of San Francisco, many thousands of Chinese people live in an area called Chinatown. The street signs give the names in both English and Chinese (right).

← 800

SACRAMENTO

唐人街

❯ COULD WE INVENT ONE LANGUAGE FOR THE WHOLE WORLD?

It's already been done! A language called Esperanto was invented over 100 years ago. Only about 100,000 people have learned to speak it fluently.

❯ WHICH IS THE LEAST SPOKEN LANGUAGE?

Fewer than 15 or 20 people in Latvia speak a language called Liv. It is 1 of around 3,000 endangered languages that may soon die out.

❯ DO WE ALL READ LEFT TO RIGHT?

The Arabic language is read right to left, and traditional Japanese top to bottom.

ARABIC CALLIGRAPHY

Arabic craftspeople often decorate buildings with calligraphy, or beautiful writing on tiles or carved in stone.

Communication

Telephones, computers, and radios allow us to keep in touch with our families and friends, or to do business with people who live on the other side of the world. A television in Los Angeles can show live images of celebrations or wars taking place in Sydney or Timbuktu.

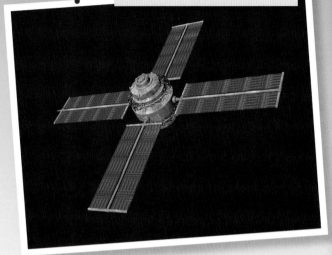

SATELLITE

Communications satellites transmit messages and images.

TOP ? QUESTION

CAN WE TALK WITHOUT WORDS?

People who are unable to hear or speak can sign with their hands. Various sign languages have been developed around the world, from China to the United States.

❯ HOW DO WE TALK THROUGH SPACE?

Satellites are machines sent into space to circle the earth. They can pick up telephone, radio, or television signals from one part of the world and beam them down to another.

❯ WHAT IS THE MOST UNUSUAL WAY TO COMMUNICATE?

In some parts of Central America, Turkey, and the Canary Islands, people worked out a way of communicating using whistles instead of words.

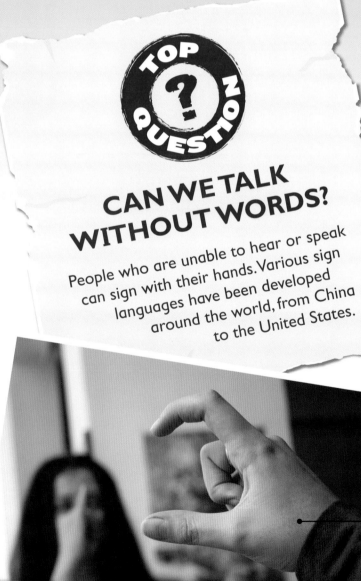

SIGN LANGUAGE

Deaf people of different nationalities can talk to each other using International Sign.

WHAT IS BODY LANGUAGE?

Movements of the head and hands can be a kind of language. Be careful! In some countries, wagging the hand palm down means "come here," but in others it means "go away." Shaking the head can mean "yes" in some countries and "no" in others.

WHAT IS E-MAIL?

E-mail, or "electronic mail," is a way of sending and receiving messages by electronic communications systems, such as computers. The first e-mail was sent in 1972.

WHAT HAS MADE THE WORLD SHRINK?

The planet hasn't really got smaller—it just seems that way. Today, telephones, e-mails, and faxes make it possible to send messages around the world instantly. Once, letters were sent by ship and took many months to arrive.

PHONES

More than 3 billion people own a cell phone and the number is growing daily.

Cities of the world >

Towns first grew up when people stopped being hunter-gatherers and learned how to farm, which meant staying in one place. The first cities were built in southwest Asia. Çatal Hüyük in Turkey was begun about 9,000 years ago. Today, more than half the world's population lives in a city.

> WHICH CITY IS NAMED AFTER A GODDESS?

Athens, the capital of Greece, shares its name with an ancient goddess named Athena. Her beautiful temple, the Parthenon, still towers over the modern city. It was built in the mid-fifth century BC.

> WHICH IS THE HIGHEST CITY?

Potosí in Bolivia stands at 13,000 feet above sea level. The city lies beneath the Cerro Rico ("Rich Mountain"), which is a source of silver ore.

POTOSÍ

The city was founded as a silver-mining town in the sixteenth century.

ATHENS

In the 1990s, Athens was one of the most polluted cities in the world. The city has now taken steps to reduce traffic fumes.

WHERE ARE THE BIGGEST CITIES IN THE WORLD?

In Japan, where big cities have spread and joined together! Japan is made up of islands that have high mountains, so most people live on the flat strips of land around the coast. In order to grow, cities have had to stretch out until they merge into each other. More than 20 million people live in the capital, Tokyo (below).

➤ WHAT PROBLEMS DO CITIES CAUSE?

Too much traffic in cities often blocks up the roads and fills the air with fumes. In some cities, there isn't enough work for everyone and some people live in poor conditions.

TOKYO

The megacity of Tokyo encompasses 26 other cities and 5 towns.

➤ WHO LIVES AT THE ENDS OF THE EARTH?

One of the world's most northerly settlements is Ny-Ålesund, in the Arctic territory of Svalbard. The southernmost city is Puerto Williams in Tierra del Fuego, Chile.

➤ WHICH COUNTRY HAS THREE CAPITALS?

The most important city in a country is called the capital. South Africa has three of them! Cape Town is the legislative capital. Pretoria is the executive capital. Bloemfontein is the judicial capital.

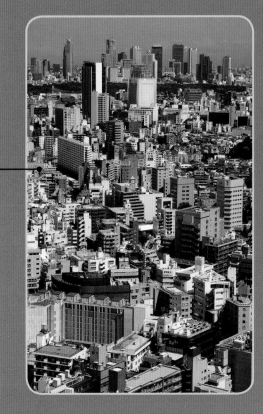

Trade and money

Throughout the ages, all kinds of things have been used as money around the world—shells, beads, and sharks' teeth. These had no value in themselves, but neither do the metal, paper, or plastic we use today. They are just tokens of exchange.

WHAT ARE CURRENCIES?

A currency is a money system, such as the Japanese yen, the U.S. dollar, the Mongolian tugrik, or the Bhutanese ngultrum. The exchange rate is what it costs to buy or sell one currency for another.

WHERE WERE BANKNOTES INVENTED?

Paper money was first used in China a thousand years ago.

WHO MAKES MONEY?

The mint—that's the place where coins and bills are made. The United States' mints in Philadelphia and Denver produce billions of new coins each year.

TOP QUESTION

WHERE IS THE SILK ROAD?

This is an ancient trading route stretching from China through Central Asia to the Mediterranean Sea. Hundreds of years ago, silk, tea, and spices were transported along this road to the West by camel trains.

› WHERE DO PEOPLE DO BUSINESS?

In Nigeria, money changes hands every day in the busy street markets. Customers haggle about the price of goods. In England, trading might take place in a big store. In Switzerland, bankers watch their computer screens to check their profits. In the New York Stock Exchange, traders grab their telephones as they buy and sell shares in companies.

› WHO CATCHES SMUGGLERS?

If you want to take some goods from one country to another, you may have to pay a tax to the government. Customs officers may check your luggage to see that you are not smuggling, or sneaking illegal goods.

COSTLY SILK

In the Middle Ages, Chinese silk was sold for great prices in Europe.

STOCK EXCHANGE

The New York Stock Exchange is over 200 years old and is the largest in the world.

Crops of the world >

The world's land is cultivated to grow crops for people to eat, while fishermen cast nets into the oceans to catch flounder, haddock, or swordfish to sell. Some climates are ideal for growing citrus fruit or sugar cane, while other regions are famous for their herds of sheep or cattle.

WHAT DO BILLIONS OF PEOPLE EAT EVERY DAY?

Billions of people eat rice every day, especially in Asia. Grains of rice are the seeds of a kind of grass that grows in flooded fields called paddies.

PADDY FIELD

Rice grows best in warm and wet river valleys.

WHERE ARE THE WORLD'S BIGGEST RANCHES?

The world's biggest sheep and cattle stations are in the Australian outback. The best way to cross these lands is in a light aircraft.

> WHAT IS A CASH CROP?

It is any crop that is sold for money. However, many small farmers around the world can only grow enough food to feed themselves and their families—there is no surplus left to sell.

WHEAT HARVEST

Combines cut the wheat and separate out the grain.

➤ WHICH WERE THE FIRST ALL-AMERICAN CROPS?

About 500 years ago, nobody in Europe had ever seen potatoes, corn, or tomatoes. These important food crops were first developed by the peoples who lived in the Americas before European settlers arrived.

TOMATO PLANT

The tomato is native to western South America. Today, it is grown worldwide.

➤ WHO ARE THE GAUCHOS?

The cowboys of the Pampas—the grasslands of Argentina. Today, the gauchos still round up the cattle on big ranches called *estancias*.

TOP QUESTION ?

WHERE ARE THE WORLD'S BREAD BASKETS?

Important wheat-producing areas are called "bread baskets," because they provide us with our bread! Wheat is a kind of grass, and it grows best in areas that were once natural grasslands, such as the prairies of the Midwest.

Transport around the world →

One of the world's most important inventions was the wheel, which developed in Mesopotamia more than 6,000 years ago. Since then, humankind has invented steam ships, cars, trains, and airplanes in order to travel the world to meet, trade, and learn.

› WHICH IS THE WORLD'S LONGEST ROAD?

The Pan-American Highway. It covers 30,000 miles, from Alaska right down to Central America. There is still a section missing in the middle, but the road starts up again and carries on through South America to Chile (below), Argentina, and Brazil.

› WHERE IS THE WORLD'S BIGGEST AIRPORT?

Riyadh airport in Saudi Arabia is bigger than some countries. It covers 88 square miles of the Arabian desert.

› WHERE ARE THE LONGEST TRUCKS?

In the outback, the dusty back country of Australia, the roads are long and straight and mostly empty. Trucks can hitch on three or four giant trailers to form a "road train."

WHERE CAN YOU CATCH A TRAIN INTO THE SKY?

In the Andes Mountains of South America. One track in Peru climbs to about 16,000 feet above sea level. In Salta, Argentina, you can catch a locomotive known as the "Train to the Clouds."

WHERE ARE BOATS USED AS BUSES?

In the beautiful Italian city of Venice, there are canals instead of roads. People travel from one part of the city to another by boat.

HOW CAN YOU TRAVEL BENEATH THE ALPS?

The Alps are snowy mountains that run across France, Italy, Switzerland, and Austria in Europe. They soar to 15,783 feet above sea level at Mont Blanc. Tunnels carry trains and cars through the mountains. The St. Gotthard tunnel in Switzerland is 10 miles long.

VENETIAN GONDOLAS

A traditional Venetian boat is called a gondola, and it is propelled by an oarsman known as a gondolier.

ROAD TRAIN

Road trains more than 160 feet long cruise the highways of Australia's outback.

Religion and culture

The World's religions

Major world religions include Islam, Hinduism, Buddhism, and Judaism. The religion with the most believers—one-third of the world's population—is Christianity. All faiths have their own beliefs about the nature of the world and special ways of praying and worshipping.

> WHERE DO YOUNG BOYS BECOME MONKS?

In Burma, a four-year-old boy learns about the life of Buddha at a special ceremony. He is dressed as a rich prince and is then given the simple robes of a Buddhist monk.

> WHICH CITY IS HOLY TO THREE FAITHS?

Jerusalem is a holy place for Jews, Muslims, and Christians. Sacred sites include the Western Wall, the Dome of the Rock, and the Church of the Holy Sepulchre.

BUDDHIST MONKS

Boy monks dressed in simple robes hold their traditional bowls ready for lunch.

> WHAT ARE PARSIS?

The Parsis belong to a sect of the Zoroastrian religion, which began long ago in ancient Persia, now Iran. Today, Parsis live in India and Pakistan.

➤ WHICH COUNTRY HAS THE MOST MUSLIMS?

Indonesia is the largest Islamic country in the world, although some parts of it, such as the island of Bali, are mostly Hindu.

JERUSALEM

Muslims worship at the Dome of the Rock in the center of Jerusalem.

WHAT IS SHINTO?

This is the ancient religion of Japan. At its holy shrines, people pray for happiness and to honor their ancestors. Many Japanese people also follow Buddhist beliefs.

EMA TABLETS

Ema tablets are covered with written wishes at a Shinto shrine in Tokyo.

A question of faith →

Most religions set down moral codes that say how believers should behave. These rules might govern how we should treat people and animals. Religious scriptures, or holy books, also tell believers how they should worship, through prayer, fasting, or pilgrimage.

❯ WHICH MONKS COVER THEIR MOUTHS?

Some monks of the Jain religion, in India, wear masks over their mouths. This is because they respect all living things and do not want to harm or swallow even the tiniest insect that might fly into their mouths.

❯ WHO WAS CONFUCIUS?

This is the English name given to the Chinese thinker Kong Fuzi (551–479 BC). His beliefs in an ordered society and respect for ancestors became very popular in China.

CONFUCIUS

Confucius taught that we must treat others as we would like to be treated.

➤ WHY DO PEOPLE FAST?

In many religions, people fast, or go without food, as part of their worship. If you visit a Muslim city, such as Cairo, during Ramadan, the ninth month of the Islamic year, you will find that no food is served during daylight hours.

➤ WHAT IS THE TAO?

Pronounced "dow," it means "the way." It is the name given to the beliefs of the Chinese thinker Lao-tzu, who lived about 2,500 years ago. Taoists believe in the harmony of the universe.

➤ WHERE DO PILGRIMS GO?

Pilgrims are religious people who travel to holy places around the world. Muslims try to travel to the sacred city of Mecca, in Saudi Arabia, at least once in their lifetime. Hindus may travel to the city of Varanasi, in India, to wash in the holy waters of the River Ganges. Some Christians travel to Bethlehem, the birthplace of Jesus Christ.

SIKH PARADE

Sikh men wearing traditional turbans hold their Kirpans, or daggers.

MECCA PILGRIMS

Muslim pilgrims ritually walk around the Kaaba ("cube") shrine, which is the holiest place in Islam.

TOP QUESTION

WHAT ARE THE FIVE "K's"?

Sikh men honor five religious traditions. Kesh is uncut hair, worn in a turban. They carry a Kangha (or comb), a Kara (or metal bangle), and a Kirpan (or dagger). They wear an undergarment called a Kaccha.

Festivals >

Religious festivals are times of special importance in the year. They often commemorate, or remember, important events in holy stories, such as the birth of Christ or the triumph of the Hindu god Krishna over demons. Festivals can be times of joy or solemn remembrance.

> WHAT IS DIWALI?

This is the time in fall when Hindus celebrate their New Year and honor Lakshmi, goddess of good fortune. Candles are lit in windows and people give each other cards and presents.

LIGHTED LAMPS

Diwali means "rows of lighted lamps." To celebrate, Hindus light small oil lamps around the home.

> WHAT IS HANUKKAH?

This Jewish festival of light lasts eight days. Families light a new candle each day on a special candlestick called a menorah (right). Hanukkah celebrates the recapture of the temple in Jerusalem in ancient times.

DIWALI

During Diwali, people light fireworks and prepare traditional meals and treats. Homes are cleaned and windows are opened.

> WHERE IS NEW YEAR'S DAY ALWAYS WET?

In Burma, people celebrate the Buddhist New Year by splashing and spraying water over their friends!

> WHEN ARE MUSLIMS ALLOWED CANDY?

The Muslim festival of Eid-ul-Fitr marks the end of a month's fasting during Ramadan. People send special cards and children enjoy eating traditional candies.

> WHERE DO DRAGONS DANCE?

Wherever Chinese people get together to celebrate their New Year, or Spring Festival. The lucky dragon weaves along the streets, held up by the people crouching underneath its long body. Firecrackers are lit to scare away evil spirits. The festival is a chance for families to get together.

DRAGON DANCE

Chinese dragons dance as drums beat and cymbals clash. The deafening noise and the fierce face of the dragon were traditionally believed to banish evil spirits on the first day of the new year.

Party time >

In every country, people like to get together at certain times of year to dance and dress up. These public parties may be in honor of particular people or they may commemorate a historical event. Sometimes they are just good reasons to practice traditional arts and music.

> WHO RIDES TO THE *FERIA*?

Each April the people of Seville, in Spain, ride on horseback to a fair by the River Guadalquivir. They wear traditional finery and dance all night.

> WHO REMEMBERS THE FIFTH OF NOVEMBER?

People in Great Britain. The date recalls the capture of Guy Fawkes, who plotted to blow up the Houses of Parliament in London in 1605. The night is marked by fireworks and blazing bonfires.

> WHO GETS TO SIT IN THE LEADER'S CHAIR?

In Turkey, April 23 is Children's Day. There are puppet shows and dances. One child gets the chance to sit at the desk of the country's prime minister!

GREEN RIVER
The Chicago River is dyed green on St. Patrick's Day.

VENETIAN MASKS
In Venice, people celebrate carnival by wearing costumes.

> WHO WEARS GREEN ON ST. PATRICK'S DAY?

St. Patrick's Day, on March 17, is the national day of Ireland. It is celebrated wherever Irish people have settled over the ages, from the United States to Australia. People wear green clothes and green shamrock leaves.

❯ WHAT IS A POW-WOW?

It means "a get-together." The Native American peoples of the United States and the First Nations of Canada meet up at pow-wows each year to celebrate their traditions with dance and music.

POW-WOW

A Native American man wearing a celebratory traditional-style outfit dances to the accompaniment of singing and drumming.

TOP QUESTION ?

WHAT IS CARNIVAL?

In ancient Rome, there was a rowdy winter festival called *saturnalia*. People copied this idea in the Middle Ages. They feasted before Lent began, when Christians had to give up eating meat. People still celebrate carnival today. In New Orleans, jazz bands parade.

The arts include painting, music, theater, and dance. Every country has its own traditional art forms, from the flamenco dancers of Spain and the opera singers of Italy to the Punch and Judy puppet shows of England.

> WHERE DO THEY DANCE LIKE THE GODS?

Kathakali is a kind of dance-drama performed in Kerala, southern India. Dancers in makeup that looks like a mask and gorgeous costumes act out ancient tales of gods and demons.

> WHO PLAYS THE PANS?

People in the Caribbean, at carnival time. The "pans" are steel drums, which can produce beautiful dance rhythms and melodies.

KATHAKALI MAKEUP

Green makeup shows that the actor is playing a noble character.

ELABORATE COSTUME

The style of costume tells the audience immediately that this character is a hero.

WHAT IS KABUKI?

Kabuki is an exciting type of drama that became popular in Japan in the 1600s and can still be seen today. The actors, who are always male, wear splendid makeup and costumes. Kabuki performances last for a whole day and feature several plays, from histories to romances.

WHERE IS STRATFORD?

There are two famous Stratfords. Four hundred years ago, Stratford-upon-Avon, in England, was the home of the great playwright William Shakespeare. The other Stratford, in Ontario, Canada, holds a drama festival in his honor.

WHO MAKES PICTURES FROM SAND?

The Navaho people of the southwestern United States make beautiful patterns using many different colored sands.

KABUKI ACTOR

As tradition demands, this male actor dressed in a kimono is playing a female role.

WHAT IS MORRIS DANCING?

Morris dancing is an English folk dance that probably dates back to the fifteenth century. The dancers bang sticks together and jingle bells tied to their legs, while stepping in time to traditional music (left).

More arts

Art can be used to express feelings and communicate ideas. Some of the oldest art forms tell stories about the earth's creation and the myths of gods and goddesses. Today, artists, musicians, dancers, and playwrights still use art to entertain, inspire, and educate us.

❯ WHERE IS THE WORLD'S OLDEST THEATER?

The oldest theater building still in use is probably the Teatro Olimpico, in Vicenza, Italy. It opened over four hundred years ago. But people were going to see plays long before that. In ancient Greece, people went to see masked actors appear in some of the funniest and saddest plays ever written, at stone open-air theaters that are sometimes used for performances today.

GAUGUIN IN RUSSIA

This 1899 painting called *Tahitian Woman with Blossom* was painted by the French artist Paul Gauguin. It hangs in the Hermitage Museum in Russia.

TAMA DRUM

The tama is beaten with a curved wooden stick.

❯ WHERE DO DRUMS TALK?

In Senegal and Gambia, in Africa, the tama is nicknamed the "talking drum." Its tightness can be varied while it is being played, making a strange throbbing sound.

? TOP QUESTION

WHERE ARE THERE 3 MILLION WORKS OF ART?

At St. Petersburg in Russia, in an art gallery made up of two great buildings, the Hermitage and the Winter Palace.

> ## WHO SINGS IN BEIJING?

Beijing opera is a spectacular performance. Musicians clash cymbals and actors sing in high voices. They take the part of heroes and villains in ancient Chinese tales. Their faces are painted and they wear beautiful costumes, some decorated with pheasant feathers.

> ## WHO DANCES A HAKA?

In New Zealand, young Maori people have kept alive many of their traditional dances. A haka was often danced by warriors to bring them strength to face battle.

> ## WHO PAINTS THE DREAMTIME?

Australia's Aborigines look back to the Dreamtime, a magical age when the world was being formed, along with its animals and peoples. Many paintings (below) show the landscape and how it was molded by animals, such as the Rainbow Serpent.

The food people eat depends not just on the crops they can grow, the animals they can raise, or the fish they can catch, but also on their traditional customs and religious beliefs. Many people in the world, for example in southern India, do not eat meat—they are vegetarian.

> WHO EATS THE MOST CHEESE?

The Greeks eat the most cheese, with the average person consuming 48 pounds every year. Three-quarters of this is feta cheese, made from ewe's and goat's milk.

> WHO MAKES THE WORLD'S HOTTEST CURRIES?

The people of southern India. A mouthwatering recipe might include fiery spices, such as red chile pepper and fresh hot green chiles, ginger, garlic, turmeric, and curry leaves.

SPICES

Spices are dried seeds, fruits, roots and barks used as flavors and preservatives.

HAGGIS

A traditional dish in Scotland is haggis with "neeps and tatties," or mashed yellow turnips and potatoes.

> WHO WROTE A POEM TO HIS HAGGIS?

Robert Burns, Scotland's greatest poet, who lived in the 1700s. The haggis is a traditional dish from Scotland made of lamb's heart, liver, and lungs, suet, onions, and oats, cooked inside— guess what—a sheep's stomach!

> WHERE DO YOU BUY MILK BY WEIGHT?

In the Russian Arctic, it is so cold in winter that milk is sold in frozen chunks rather than by the gallon.

HOW DO WE KEEP FOOD FRESH?

Today, butter can be sent across the world, kept cool by refrigeration. The first ever refrigerator ship was invented in 1876 to carry beef from Argentina. But how did people keep food fresh before that? The old methods were simpler— pickling, smoking, or drying. Traditional methods are still used today to produce some of the world's tastiest foods, such as Japanese pickles (below).

World delicacies

Sushi is considered a great delicacy in Japan. In the United States, many people think there is nothing tastier than roast beef. The food we like is a question of personal taste. Sheep's eyeballs and pigs' ears are considered to be the yummiest delicacies somewhere in the world!

> WHAT IS JAMBALAYA?

Rice and peppers with meat or shrimp, all in an amazing hot, spicy sauce. Where is this served up? New Orleans, in the steamy south.

SUSHI

In Japan, sushi is rice wrapped in sheets of seaweed and often topped with meat, fish, or vegetables.

CAVIAR

Black caviar is the salted eggs of the sturgeon fish, while red caviar is the eggs of the salmon. Both varieties are considered a great delicacy.

> WHAT IS CAVIAR?

One of the most expensive foods in the world. It is made of eggs from a fish called the sturgeon, which lives in lakes and rivers in Russia and other northern lands.

> WHAT IS YERBA MATÉ?

It is a bitter but refreshing hot drink, made from the leaves of the Paraguay holly. It is sipped from a gourd (a kind of pumpkin shell) through a silver straw, and is very popular in Argentina.

CAN YOU EAT SEAWEED?

Various seaweeds are eaten in Japan, and in South Wales, in Great Britain, seaweed is used in a dish called laverbread. A seaweed called carrageen moss is often used to thicken ice cream.

❯ WHO EATS SPIDERS?

Spiders are a delicacy in Cambodia. The tastiest are plucked straight from their burrow and fried with plenty of garlic and salt.

❯ WHO INVENTED NOODLES?

Which noodles came first—Italian spaghetti or Chinese lo mein? Some people say that the traveler Marco Polo brought the secret of noodlemaking back to Italy from China in the Middle Ages. Others say the Romans were making pasta in Italy long before that.

SINGAPORE NOODLES

Singapore noodles are a tasty mix of shrimp, red peppers, eggs, and seasoning.

Clothes of the World

We are so used to wearing clothes that we rarely think about why we wear them! People wear clothes to protect themselves from the weather, for modesty, and for comfort. We also choose our clothes to reflect who we are.

TUAREG DRESS

The Tuareg of the Sahara cover their heads to keep out sun and sand.

WHERE DO PANAMA HATS COME FROM?

Actually, Panama hats were first made in Ecuador, where they were braided from the leaves of the toquilla palm. But they were first exported, or shipped abroad, from Panama.

HOW DO PEOPLE DRESS IN HOT COUNTRIES?

In hot countries, people protect their heads from the sun with broad-brim hats, from the Mexican sombrero to the cone-shape hats worn by farm workers in southern China and Vietnam.

WHAT ARE CLOTHES MADE FROM?

Clothes today may be made from natural fibers, such as wool or cotton, or from artificial fibers, such as nylon and plastic.

BATIK

Intricately patterned batik cloth is made in Java, Indonesia.

WHAT IS BATIK?

This is a way of making pretty patterns on cloth. Wax is put on the fiber so that the dye sinks in only in certain places. This method was invented in Southeast Asia. In Indonesia, batik is considered a national art form and patterns are handed down over generations of craftspeople.

HOW DO WE KEEP WARM AND DRY?

Since prehistoric times, people have used fur and animal skins to keep out the cold. Today, clothing for polar expeditions uses wool and feathers, plus man-made fibers that are very warm but not too heavy.

PARIS FASHION SHOW

People from all over the world go to see the beautiful fashions.

TOP QUESTION ?

WHERE IS THE CAPITAL OF FASHION?

Milan, London, New York, and many other cities stage fantastic fashion shows each year. But Paris, in France, has been the center of world fashion for hundreds of years.

National costumes

Most people today wear T-shirts and jeans, skirts, or suits. Only on special occasions do they still put on traditional regional costumes. But in some countries, people still wear local dress regularly. This might be the elaborate kimono of Japan or the colorful sari of India.

WHO WEARS FEATHERS TO A SINGSING?

A singsing is a big festival in Papua New Guinea. Men paint their faces and wear ornaments of bone and shell, and long bird-of-paradise feathers. Traditional dress may include skirts made of leaves and grass.

WHICH LADIES WEAR TALL LACE HATS?

The Breton people of northwest France are proud of their costume, which they wear for special occasions. The men wear vests and big black hats. The women wear lace caps, some of which are high and shaped like chimneys.

WHO ARE THE TRUE CLOGGIES?

A hundred years ago clogs, or wooden shoes, were worn in many parts of Europe. The most famous clogs were the Dutch ones (above), which are still worn today by farmers and market traders in the Netherlands.

SILK WEAVING

Beautiful silk is still woven by hand in some parts of Asia.

TOP QUESTION

WHO INVENTED SILK?

The Chinese were the first people to make silk, from the cocoons of silkworms, thousands of years ago. Today, silk may be used to make bright Indian wraps called saris and Japanese robes called kimonos.

GREEK EVZÓNES

Guards at the Greek President's palace wear uniforms that date back to the nineteenth century.

❯ WHERE DO SOLDIERS WEAR SKIRTS?

Guards of honor in the Greek army are called Evzónes. Their uniform is based on the old-fashion costume of the mountain peoples—a white skirt, woolen tights, and a cap with a tassel.

Homes around the world >

Houses must shelter people from cold and heat, rain and snow, storms and floods. Around the world, people have come up with different solutions for building their homes, depending on the materials they have to build with and the weather conditions that they face.

> WHY DO PEOPLE LIVE UNDERGROUND?

To stay cool! At Coober Pedy in Australia, it is so hot that miners digging for opals built houses and even a church underground. These rock homes remain at a constant temperature all year.

> WHAT ARE HOUSES LIKE IN THE ARCTIC?

Today, the Inuit people of Canada live in houses, huts, and tents. Traditionally, they lived in igloos made out of blocks of snow. Igloos are still used today by Inuits on the move.

> WHAT ARE HOUSES MADE FROM?

Mud, stone, slate, rocks, bricks, branches, reeds, steel girders, sheets of iron, concrete, glass, straw, turf, ice, bamboo, animal hides, cardboard boxes—you name it! All over the world, people make use of whatever materials they can find or produce to build homes. A building made of stone can remain standing for thousands of years, while wooden or hide houses may be rebuilt frequently.

IGLOO
Snow blocks are stacked into a sturdy dome shape.

LAKE TITICACA

Reed homes are built on floating islands made of reeds!

WHY DO CHALETS HAVE BIG ROOFS?

In the mountains of Switzerland, the wooden houses have broad roofs, designed for heavy snowfalls each winter.

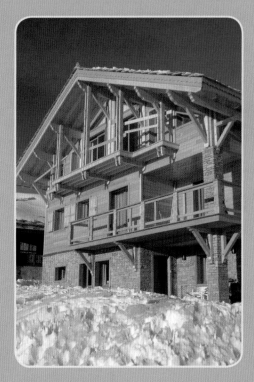

➤ WHY BUILD REED HOUSES?

It makes sense to use the nearest building material available. Tall reeds grow around Lake Titicaca in Peru, so the Indians who live there use them to build their beautiful houses.

➤ WHY ARE HOUSES BUILT ON STILTS?

In many parts of the world, homes are built on stilts to protect them from flooding or to stop animals from running into the house.

WARM AS SNOW

Snow is an excellent insulator, so igloos are surprisingly warm inside, particularly when heated by a stove.

Somewhere to live →

Modern buildings look much the same wherever they have been built, from Los Angeles to Singapore. But all types of local houses can still be seen as well, from mud huts or homes carved from rock to the tents of the Bedouin nomads.

WHERE DO PEOPLE LIVE IN FAIRY CHIMNEYS?

In Cappadocia in eastern Turkey, people have carved homes out of natural cone-shape rock formations known as "fairy chimneys."

WHERE IS THE BLUE CITY?

The Indian city of Jodhpur is known as the "Blue City" because many of its houses are painted blue (right). The inhabitants believe the color reflects heat and keeps away mosquitoes.

WHERE DO THEY BUILD MUD HUTS?

Thatched huts with walls of dried mud can still be seen in parts of Africa, such as Mali. They are cheap to build, cool to live in, and often look beautiful, too.

CAPPADOCIA

The tall "chimneys" are caused by erosion over thousands of years.

ROCK HOMES

The rocks are hollowed to create homes and churches.

> WHICH PEOPLE LIVE IN CARAVANS?

Many of Europe's Roma people live in caravans, moving from one campsite to another. The Roma, who are sometimes called Gypsies, arrived in Europe from India about 500 years ago.

> WHY WERE SKYSCRAPERS INVENTED?

So that more people could fit into a small area of city. High-rise apartments and offices were first built in Chicago about 120 years ago. Newly invented elevators saved people a long climb!

TOP QUESTION

WHY DO PEOPLE LIVE IN TENTS?

In many parts of the world, there are people who do not live in the same place all year round. Instead, they follow their herds of sheep and goats from one pasture to another. Such people are called nomads. The Bedouin are nomads who live in North Africa. Their tents are woven from camel hair (below).

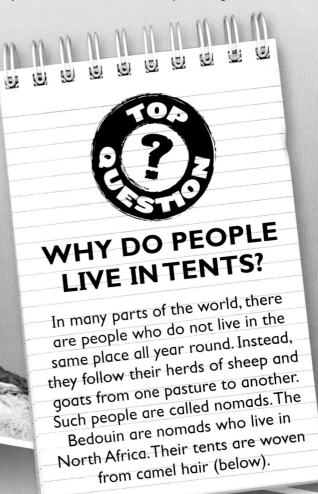

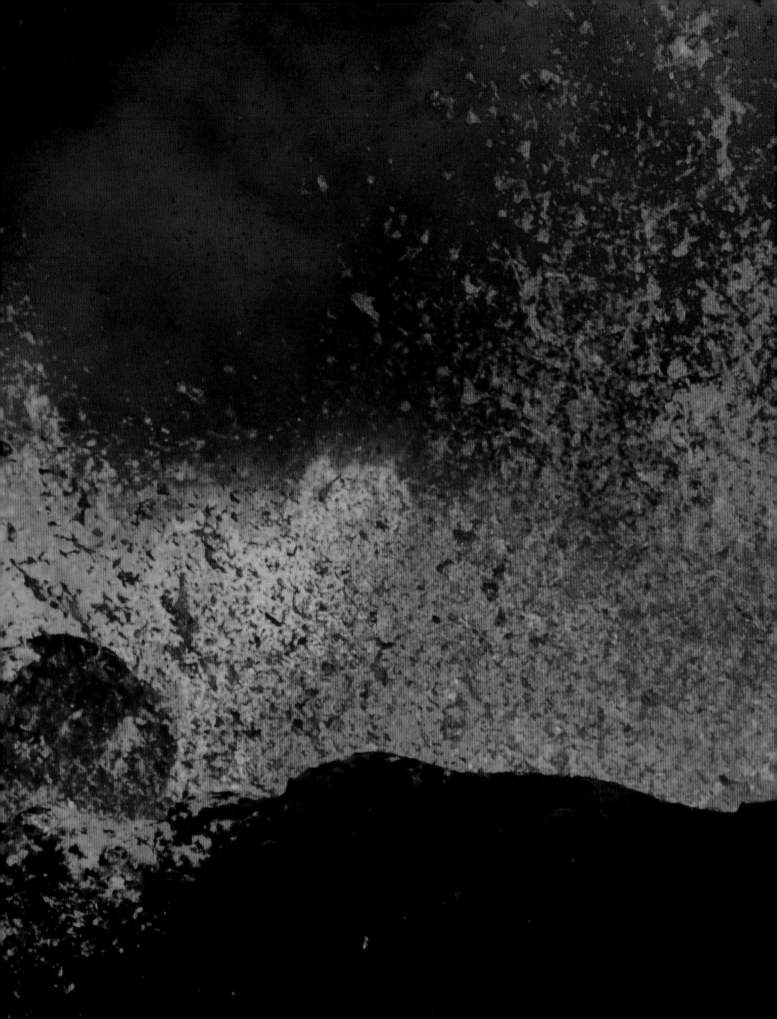

Planet earth

Earth's history >

HOW IS THE EARTH'S HISTORY DIVIDED?

Scientists divide the last 590 million years into three eras: the Paleozoic (meaning old life), Mesozoic (middle life), and Cenozoic (new life). The earth's history before the Paleozoic era is divided into three eons: the Hadean, Archean, and Proterozoic (see diagram below).

OUR PLANET'S BIRTH

The earth formed 4.6 billion years ago, but conditions were not ready for life until 800 million years later.

WHAT ARE PERIODS AND EPOCHS?

The geological eras are subdivided into periods, such as the Jurassic. Periods are divided into epochs, such as the Pleistocene.

Humans have only been on the earth for about 100,000 years. But scientists can form a picture of our planet's history before humans existed by studying the earth's rocks and fossils. We have discovered when the earliest life forms emerged and what the first animals looked like.

TIME LINE

This time line shows the earth's history.

HADEAN	ARCHEAN				PROTEROZOIC									
	Eoarchean	Paleo-archean	Meso-archean	Neo-archean	Paleoproterozoic				Mesoproterozoic			Neoproterozoic		
					Siderian	Rhyacian	Orosirian	Statherian	Calymmian	Ectasian	Stenian	Tonian	Cryogenian	Ediacaran

| 4,600 | 3,800 | 3,600 | 3,200 | 2,800 | 2,500 | 2,300 | 2,050 | 1,800 | 1,600 | 1,400 | 1,200 | 1,000 | 850 | 630 | 542 |

Millions of years ago

❯ WHAT DID EARLY ANIMALS LOOK LIKE?

By around 500 million years ago, bacteria in the oceans had evolved into the earliest fish. These strange creatures had no jaws—they had funnel-like sucking mouths.

EARLY LIFE

Stromatolites form when bacteria builds up solid mats of calcium carbonate, also known as lime.

TOP QUESTION ?

WHAT ARE STROMATOLITES?

Primitive life forms may have first appeared on the earth about 3,800 million years ago. These bacteria lived in the oceans and formed deposits called stromatolites. Today, modern stromatolites can be seen in shallow seas (left).

❯ WHY WASN'T THERE LIFE ON EARTH RIGHT AWAY?

The earth's surface was probably molten for many millions of years after its formation. Life first began in the oceans, and these did not exist for the first 400–800 million years.

❯ WHEN DID PLANTS START TO GROW ON LAND?

The first land plants appeared in the Silurian period. These simple plants reproduced by releasing spores. Plants produced oxygen and provided food for the first land animals—amphibians. Amphibians first developed in the Devonian period from fish whose fins had evolved into limbs.

PHANEROZOIC															
Paleozoic						Mesozoic			Cenozoic						
Cambrian	Ordovician	Silurian	Devonian	Carboniferous	Permian	Triassic	Jurassic	Cretaceous	Paleogene			Neogene		Quaternary	
									Paleocene	Eocene	Oligocene	Miocene	Pliocene	Pleisto-cene	Holo-cene
542	488.3	443.7	416	359.2	299	251	199.6	145.5	65.5	55.8	33.9	23	5.3	1.8	0.01 0

Millions of years ago

Evolving life >

Humans are descended from the bacteria that were the earth's earliest life forms. Evolution is the process of how life forms change over the course of generations. When an animal develops a successful new feature—such as the ability to walk on two legs—this trait is passed down to future generations.

> WHY DID DINOSAURS BECOME EXTINCT?

The dinosaurs died out at the end of the Cretaceous period, 65 million years ago. Many experts believe that this happened when an enormous asteroid struck the earth. The impact threw up a huge cloud of dust, which blocked out the sunlight for a long time. Land plants died and so the dinosaurs starved to death.

FOSSIL FISH

This fish, with a visible backbone, lived in Devonian times.

> WHAT WERE THE FIRST ANIMALS WITH BACKBONES?

Jawless fish were the first animals with backbones. They appeared during the Ordovician period. Fish with skeletons of cartilage, such as sharks, first appeared in the Devonian period.

> WHY IS THE CAMBRIAN PERIOD IMPORTANT?

Before the Cambrian period, most living creatures were soft-bodied and left few fossils. During the Cambrian period, many creatures had hard parts, which were preserved as fossils in layers of rock—ready for scientists to study later!

❯ WHEN DID MAMMALS FIRST APPEAR?

Mammals lived on the earth from at least the start of the Jurassic period. But they did not become common until after the extinction of the dinosaurs.

DEINONYCHUS

The meat-eating dinosaur *Deinonychus* had sharp teeth and a strong jaw, so it could seize and devour its prey.

HOMINID

This hominid skull is over 3 million years old.

❯ WHEN DID PEOPLE FIRST LIVE ON EARTH?

Hominids (apelike creatures that walked upright) first appeared on the earth over 4 million years ago. Modern humans appeared about 100,000 years ago.

❯ WHO WERE THE NEANDERTHALS?

Neanderthals were relatives of modern humans that disappeared 24,000 years ago. Some scientists believe that they did not die out—they may have bred with modern humans and could be among our ancestors!

The earth's plates

The surface of the earth may appear solid but it's actually like a giant jigsaw puzzle. The planet's outer layers are divided into plates that float on a partly molten layer of rock. Currents in the molten rock slowly move the plates around. Over millions of years, the movement of these plates can create huge mountain ranges.

WHAT IS THE EARTH'S MANTLE?

The mantle is a partly molten rocky shell that is about 1,800 miles thick. It makes up 70 percent of the Earth's volume. The mantle surrounds the earth's iron-rich core. Surrounding the mantle is the earth's crust, on which we live. It is a thin layer of crystallized products, formed by melting and movement within the mantle.

WHAT ARE PLATES?

The earth's hard outer layers are divided into large blocks called plates. These consist of the earth's crust and the top part of the mantle.

HOW DEEP ARE PLATES?

There are about seven large plates. Their exact thickness is uncertain, but they could be up to 90 miles in places.

GROWING PEAKS

The mountains rise by 1/5 of an inch a year.

THE HIMALAYAS

The Himalayas started to form when plates collided about 50 million years ago.

CAN PLATES MOVE SIDEWAYS?

Yes. Plates can move apart, push against each other, or move sideways along huge cracks in the ground called transform faults.

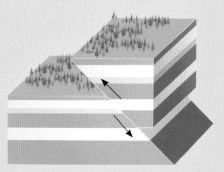

Plates push against each other

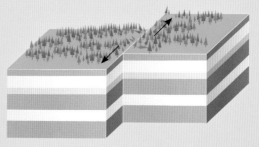

Plates move sideways (transform fault)

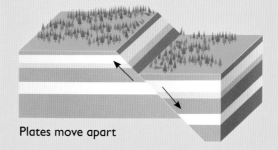

Plates move apart

PLATE BOUNDARIES

This diagram shows the seven major and many minor plates that cover the earth.

❯ HOW FAST DO PLATES MOVE?

Plates move, on average, between 1 ½ and 3 inches a year. This may sound slow but, over millions of years, these small plate movements dramatically change the face of the earth.

❯ WHAT HAPPENS WHEN PLATES COLLIDE?

If this happens along a deep trench beneath an ocean, one plate is pulled beneath another and is melted and recycled. On land, when continents collide, their edges are squeezed up into new mountain ranges.

Continental drift ➤

The continents—Europe, the Americas, Africa, Australia, Asia, and Antarctica—lie on different plates. The plates constantly move, slowly changing the face of the earth. This movement of the continents is called continental drift.

220 million years ago

155 million years ago

60 million years ago

❯ HAS EARTH ALWAYS LOOKED THE SAME?

No. If aliens had visited the earth 200 million years ago, they would have seen only one huge continent, called Pangaea, surrounded by one ocean. Around 180 million years ago, Pangaea began to break up. By 100 million years ago, plates supporting India, Australia, and Antarctica were drifting away from Africa, and North America was moving away from Europe.

❯ ARE THE CONTINENTS STILL MOVING?

Africa is moving northward into Europe at the rate of a few fractions of an inch a year. The Americas are moving farther from Africa.

❯ WHO FIRST SUGGESTED THE IDEA OF CONTINENTAL DRIFT?

In the early 1900s, an American, F. B. Taylor, and a German, Alfred Wegener, both suggested the idea of continental drift. But scientists could not explain how the plates moved until the 1960s, following studies of the ocean floor.

HAWAIIAN ISLANDS

A volcanic cone rises behind Waikiki beach in Hawaii.

TOP ? QUESTION

HOW IS CONTINENTAL DRIFT MEASURED?

A global network of observation stations measures the time taken for lasers to bounce back from satellites. This provides exact measurements of where the continents are and how they are moving.

❯ HAVE FOSSILS HELPED TO PROVE CONTINENTAL DRIFT?

Fossils of animals that could not have swum across oceans have been found in different continents. This suggests that the continents were once all joined together and that animals could walk from one continent to another.

LASER TRACKING

A laser at the McDonald Observatory in Texas, tracks the drift of the continents.

❯ HOW WAS HAWAII FORMED?

Hawaii's existence proves that continental drift takes place! The Hawaiian islands were created as the Pacific Plate drifted to the northwest. As it moved, the plate passed over a hot spot in the mantle and a series of new volcanoes was punched up through the surface, one after another. Each of the islands in the Hawaiian chain has a volcano.

Earthquakes ➤

Earthquakes happen when the earth's plates move in a sudden jerk, shaking the ground. Powerful earthquakes can make buildings wobble and collapse. Earthquakes on mountains can cause landslides that sometimes destroy towns in the valleys below.

➤ WHERE ARE EARTHQUAKES LIKELY TO HAPPEN?

The most violent earthquakes occur around the edges of the plates that make up the earth's outer layers. For most of the time, the plates' edges are jammed together. But gradually currents under the plates build up, increasing pressure, and the plates move in a jerk. This shakes all the rocks around it, setting off an earthquake.

➤ DO EARTHQUAKES AND VOLCANOES OCCUR IN THE SAME PLACES?

Yes, most active volcanoes occur near the edges of moving plates. Earthquakes are common in these regions, too.

➤ WHAT IS A TSUNAMI?

Earthquakes on the seabed trigger waves called tsunamis. Tsunamis travel through the water at up to 500 miles an hour. As they approach land, the water piles up into deadly waves many feet high.

SAN FRANCISCO QUAKE

In 1906, half of San Francisco's buildings were destroyed by an earthquake.

TOP QUESTION

WHAT IS THE SAN ANDREAS FAULT?

The San Andreas fault is a long transform fault (see p. 93) in California. Movements along this plate edge have caused huge earthquakes in the cities of San Francisco and Los Angeles.

SICHUAN QUAKE

In 2008, an earthquake hit Sichuan province in China, leaving more than 69,000 people dead.

> CAN SCIENTISTS PREDICT EARTHQUAKES?

In 1975, Chinese scientists correctly predicted an earthquake using a seismograph (left) to measure plate movements. They saved the lives of many people. But scientists have not yet found an absolutely certain way of forecasting earthquakes, so fatalities and injuries regularly occur as a result of quakes around the world.

Volcanoes

Volcanoes erupt when hot molten rock from deep down in the earth's mantle rises through the earth's hard outer layers and reaches the surface. The molten rock is called magma, but when it reaches the surface it is called lava. Most volcanoes occur near the edges of plates.

WHAT ARE HOT SPOTS?

Some volcanoes lie far from plate edges. They form over "hot spots," areas of great heat in the earth's mantle. Hawaii in the Pacific Ocean is over a hot spot.

DO ALL VOLCANOES ERUPT IN THE SAME WAY?

Volcanoes can explode upward or sideways, or erupt "quietly." Trapped inside the magma in explosive volcanoes are gases and water vapor. These gases splatter the magma and hurl columns of volcanic ash and dust into the air. Sometimes clouds of ash and gas are shot sideways out of volcanoes. In "quietly" erupting volcanoes, magma emerges as runny lava and flows downhill.

LAVA BURST

Lava erupts from a central vent and burns everything in its path as it flows downhill.

WHAT ARE HOT SPRINGS AND GEYSERS?

These are places where underground water, heated by magma inside the earth, breaks through to the surface. Warm water bubbles up at hot springs. Geysers hurl boiling water and steam into the air.

WHAT IS AN EXTINCT VOLCANO?

Volcanoes that have not erupted in recorded history are said to be "extinct." This means that scientists think they will not erupt again.

WHAT IS A DORMANT VOLCANO?

Some active volcanoes erupt only now and then. When they are not erupting, they are said to be dormant, or sleeping.

DO VOLCANOES DO ANY GOOD?

Volcanic eruptions cause tremendous damage, but soil formed from volcanic ash is extremely fertile. Volcanic rocks are also used in building and chemical industries.

GEYSER

Eruptions at the Lady Knox geyser in New Zealand create a water jet 65 feet high.

POMPEIIAN

The volcano Vesuvius erupted in AD 79, burying the town of Pompeii in volcanic ash. This victim was buried before he or she could escape.

99

Rocks and minerals >

Minerals are solids that are formed naturally in the earth. A common mineral is quartz. Like all minerals, it has a crystal structure— a symmetrical shape like that of a snowflake. Rocks are made of a mixture of minerals. Sandstone and limestone both contain quartz.

> WHAT ARE ELEMENTS AND MINERALS?

The earth's crust contains 92 elements. The two most common elements are oxygen and silicon. Some minerals, such as gold, occur in a pure state. But most minerals are chemical combinations of elements. For example, minerals made of oxygen and silicon, such as quartz, are called silicates.

> WHAT ARE THE THREE MAIN KINDS OF ROCK?

There are igneous, sedimentary, and metamorphic rocks. Igneous rocks, such as basalt and granites, are formed from cooled magma. Many sedimentary rocks are made from worn fragments of other rocks. For example, sandstone is formed from sand. Sand consists mainly of quartz, a mineral found in granite. Metamorphic rocks are changed by heat and pressure. For example, great heat turns limestone into marble.

> WHAT ARE THE MOST COMMON ROCKS?

Sedimentary rocks cover 75 percent of the earth's land surface. But igneous rocks make up 95 percent of the rocks in the top 10 miles of the earth's crust.

CHALK CLIFFS

England's White Cliffs of Dover are formed of the sedimentary rock chalk.

➤ WHAT ARE THE MOST VALUABLE MINERALS?

Gemstones, such as diamonds, rubies, sapphires, and emeralds, are valuable minerals. Gold and silver are regarded as minerals, too, although they occur as pure elements.

GOLD NUGGETS

Precious gold nuggets and grains appear in rocks and soil.

➤ WHAT IS CONGLOMERATE?

It is a sedimentary rock made of a mixture of different-size pebbles cemented together by sand. It is formed in river channels over thousands of years.

COAL MINE

Coal is often mined deep under the ground and is burned as fuel around the world.

TOP QUESTION

IS COAL A ROCK?

No. Although coal is sometimes called an organic rock, it is not a real rock because rocks are inorganic (lifeless). Coal, like oil and natural gas, was formed millions of years ago from the remains of once-living things. That is why coal, oil, and gas are called fossil fuels.

People have been making use of rocks and minerals for millennia. Rock is used for building, from the sandstone of the Egyptian Pyramids to the limestone of St. Paul's Cathedral in London. Minerals are needed everywhere from jewelry to industry, where diamonds are used to cut other materials.

> WHAT ARE BIRTHSTONES?

Birthstones are minerals that symbolize the month of a person's birth. For example, garnet is the birthstone for January, while ruby is the stone for people born in July.

> CAN MINERALS MAKE YOU INVISIBLE?

No, although in the Middle Ages people thought that you would become invisible if you wore an opal wrapped in a bay leaf.

AMETHYST

Amethyst is the birthstone for people born in February.

> WHAT IS THE HARDEST MINERAL?

Diamond, a pure but rare form of carbon, is formed under great pressure deep inside the earth. It is the hardest natural substance.

MINING

Diamonds are mined around the globe, but about half the world's diamonds come from Africa.

➤ WHAT COMMON ROCKS ARE USED FOR BUILDINGS?

Two sedimentary rocks, limestone and sandstone, and the igneous rock granite are all good building stones. The metamorphic rock marble is often used to decorate buildings.

MARBLE

The Acropolis in Athens is constructed from marble.

➤ ARE SOME MINERALS MORE PLENTIFUL THAN OTHERS?

Many useful minerals are abundant. Other important minerals are in limited supply and are often recycled from scrap. Recycling saves energy, which has to be used to heat and filter metal ores, such as iron, to get the pure metal.

CARYATIDS

Marble is ideal for carvings, such as these fifth century BC caryatids, or female figures.

➤ WHICH IS THE WORLD'S LARGEST GEMSTONE?

Many jewels compete for this title. It may be an emerald that is 49 inches long and weighs 1,180 pounds—that's the weight of about seven men!

DIAMONDS

Gems are measured in carats, which are equal to seven one-thousandth of an ounce. A 1 carat diamond may cost up to $40,000.

Fossils >

Fossils are the impressions of ancient life preserved in rocks. When creatures die, their remains are often slowly buried in sand or soil. Their soft parts usually rot, but the hard parts, such as bones, teeth, and shells, can be preserved as minerals or molds in the rock.

> WHAT ARE TRACE FOSSILS?

Trace fossils give information about animals that lived in ancient times. Animal burrows are sometimes preserved, giving scientists clues about the creatures that made them. Other trace fossils include footprints.

> HOW ARE FOSSILS TURNED TO STONE?

When tree trunks or bones are buried, minerals deposited from water sometimes replace the original material. The wood or bone is then petrified, or turned to stone.

> WHAT IS AN AMMONITE?

Ammonites were sea-dwelling mollusks, related to squid. Fossils of ammonites are common in rocks of the Mesozoic era.

DINOSAUR PRINTS

Footprints can be preserved when the mud in which they are made quickly hardens and then is buried under more mud.

TRILOBITES

Trilobites were very common in the seas of the Paleozoic era.

➤ HAS FLESH EVER BEEN PRESERVED AS A FOSSIL?

In Siberia, woolly mammoths, which lived more than 40,000 years ago, sank in swampy ground. When the soil froze, their complete bodies were preserved in the icy subsoil.

➤ WHICH IS THE OLDEST FOSSIL INSECT EVER FOUND?

This is a 400-million-year-old creature known as *Rhyniognatha hirsti*. It was found in Scotland in 1919. The insect is believed to have had wings, making it one of the earliest known creatures to take to the air.

TOP QUESTION

WHAT IS AMBER?

Amber is a hard substance formed from the sticky resin of trees. Tiny animals were sometimes trapped in the resin. Their bodies were preserved when the resin hardened.

SPEED AND SIZE

Studying dinosaur tracks can tell scientists about the length of the animal's legs and the speed at which it was moving.

FOSSIL FLIES

These flies were trapped in sticky resin millions of years ago.

More fossils →

Paleontologists study fossils to discover what prehistoric animals looked like and how they might have survived. Examining the fossils of plants has allowed scientists to build up a picture of how the world may have looked millions of years ago.

❯ HOW ARE FOSSILS DATED?

Dead creatures are found buried under volcanic ash. The ash can contain radioactive substances that scientists can date. In this way, they can work out the time when the animals lived.

❯ WHAT IS CARBONIZATION?

Leaves usually rot after plants die. But sometimes they are buried by mud on lake beds. Sediments around the leaf are gradually compressed into rock. Over time, bacteria change the chemistry of the leaf until only the carbon it contains remains. The shape of the leaf is preserved in the rock as a carbon smear.

FOSSIL LEAVES

The imprints of these leaves have been carbonized.

WHAT CAN SCIENTISTS LEARN FROM FOSSILS?

From the study of fossils, known as paleontology, scientists can learn about how living things evolved on the earth. Fossils can also help paleontologists to date rocks. This is because some species lived for only a short period on the earth. So, if the fossils of these creatures are found in rocks in different places, the rocks must have been formed at the same time. Such fossils are called index fossils.

BITE SIZE

Prehistoric sharks' teeth, such as those of *Auriculatus*, *Megalodon*, and *Otodus obliquus*, tell scientists what sharks might have eaten.

WHAT IS A PETRIFIED LOG?

Petrified logs were formed when water replaced the molecules in buried logs with minerals. Slowly, stone replicas of the logs were produced. The Petrified Forest National Park in Arizona is one of the world's largest and most colorful concentrations of petrified wood.

PILTDOWN MAN

The identity of the famous Piltdown hoaxer remains unknown to this day.

WHAT WAS PILTDOWN MAN?

Some bones, thought to be fossils of an early human ancestor, were discovered at Piltdown Common, England, between 1910 and 1912. But Piltdown Man was a fake. The skull was human, but the jawbone came from an orang-utan.

Earth extremes >

Over billions of years, constant movement and heat beneath the earth's surface has created vast mountain ranges and towering volcanoes. Oceans crash onto wide bays, while rivers snake across continents. These extremes are part of what makes our planet such an extraordinary home.

> WHICH IS THE LARGEST HIGH PLATEAU?

The immense, windswept Tibetan Plateau in China covers about 720,000 square miles.

> WHICH IS THE LARGEST RIVER BASIN?

The Amazon River Basin in South America covers about 2,750,000 square miles. The Madeira River, which flows into the Amazon, is the world's longest tributary, at 2,100 miles.

WHICH IS THE DEEPEST LAKE?

Lake Baikal, in Siberia, eastern Russia, is the world's deepest lake. The deepest spot measured so far is 5,375 feet.

VAST AREA

The plateau is about four times the size of France and has an average height of 15,000 feet.

➤ WHICH IS THE LARGEST ISLAND?

Greenland covers 836,000 square miles. (Geographers consider Australia to be a continent and not an island.)

➤ WHICH IS THE TALLEST VOLCANO?

It's Mauna Kea in Hawaii. It is both the world's tallest mountain and tallest volcano, but 19,000 feet of it lies under the Pacific Ocean.

➤ WHICH IS THE LARGEST BAY?

Hudson Bay in Canada covers an area of about 480,000 square miles. It is linked to the North Atlantic Ocean by the Hudson Strait.

AMAZON BASIN

The Amazon Basin lies in six different countries.

LAKE BAIKAL

The lake holds more water than all five of the North American Great Lakes combined.

On our amazing planet, we can climb 29,000 feet high to the summit of Mount Everest or descend 5,250 feet beneath the surface in the world's deepest cave. We can sail on the planet's widest lake or journey across the largest continent.

TOP QUESTION ?

WHICH IS THE LONGEST RIVER?

The Nile in northeast Africa is 4,109 miles long. The second longest river, the Amazon in South America, discharges 60 times more water than the Nile.

> WHICH IS THE LARGEST INLAND BODY OF WATER OR LAKE?

The salty Caspian Sea, which lies partly in Europe and partly in Asia, has an area of about 145,000 square miles. The largest freshwater lake is Lake Superior, one of the Great Lakes of North America. Lake Superior has an area of about 32,000 square miles.

> WHICH IS THE LOWEST POINT ON LAND?

The shoreline of the Dead Sea, between Israel and Jordan, is 1,300 feet below the sea level of the Mediterranean Sea.

> WHICH IS THE DEEPEST CAVE?

The Réseau Jean Bernard in France is the deepest cave network. It reaches a depth of 5,250 feet.

THE DEAD SEA

This inland lake is nearly nine times saltier than the ocean.

> WHICH IS THE BIGGEST CONTINENT?

Asia covers an area of 17,139,000 square miles. The other continents are Africa (11,677,000 square miles), North America (9,362,000 square miles), South America (6,880,000 square miles), Antarctica (5,500,000 square miles), Europe (3,998,000 square miles), and Australia (2,968,000 square miles).

LIGHTHOUSE

Around 50 lighthouses warn sailors along Lake Superior's 2,700 miles of coast.

> WHICH IS THE BIGGEST OCEAN?

The Pacific Ocean is the world's largest. It covers one-third of the earth's surface, with an area of 70 million square miles. The world has four other oceans, in descending order of size: Atlantic, Indian, Southern, and Arctic.

LAKE SUPERIOR

Over 200 rivers flow into the lake, which is drained by St. Mary's River.

The earth's changing face

Weathering ➤

There are two forms of weathering. Physical weathering is the breakdown of rocks through contact with atmospheric conditions, such as heat, water, ice, and pressure. Chemical weathering is caused by chemicals naturally occurring in the atmosphere.

WEATHERING ROCK

Rocks, especially limestone, are chemically weathered by the action of rainwater.

➤ HOW QUICKLY IS THE LAND WORN AWAY?

An average of almost 1½ inches is worn away from land areas every 1,000 years. Over millions of years, mountains can be worn down to plains.

➤ WHAT IS GROUNDWATER?

Groundwater is water that seeps slowly through rocks, such as sandstones and limestones. The top level of the water in the rocks is called the water table. Wells are dug down into the water table.

➤ HOW DOES WATER WEATHER ROCKS?

Water dissolves rock salt. It also reacts with some types of the hard rock granite, turning minerals in the rock into a clay called kaolin.

> CAN THE SUN CAUSE WEATHERING?

In dry regions, rocks are heated by the sun, but they cool at night. These changes crack rock surfaces, which peel away.

TOP QUESTION ?

WHAT ARE SPRINGS?

Springs occur when groundwater flows to the surface. Springs are the sources of many rivers. Hot springs often occur in volcanic areas, where the groundwater is heated by magma.

> HOW IS LIMESTONE WEATHERED?

Limestone is worn away by chemical weathering. Limestone consists mostly of calcium carbonate, which reacts with rainwater. Over time, the rainwater slowly dissolves the limestone.

LIMESTONE CLIFFS

The extraordinary limestone cliffs around Guilin in China were created by limestone weathering.

More weathering →

Once weathering has broken down a rock, the materials left over can form soil, in which plants take root. Weathering also creates some of the earth's most beautiful natural features.

❱ HOW DO LIVING THINGS WEATHER ROCKS?

Rocks can be exposed by burrowing animals and then weathered. Bacteria can also help to weather rocks.

❱ WHAT ARE STALACTITES AND STALAGMITES?

Water containing calcium carbonate drips down from the ceilings of limestone caves. The water gradually deposits calcium carbonate to form hanging, icicle-like structures called stalactites. Stalagmites are columns of calcium carbonate deposited by dripping water, but stalagmites grow upward from the floors of caves.

STALAGMITES

Stalagmites grow upward from the floors of caves, while stalactites (top) grow downward.

➤ HOW DOES FROST BREAK UP ROCKS?

At night in the mountains, people may hear sounds like gunshots. These are made by rocks being split apart by frost action (an example of physical weathering). As the water in cracks in the rocks freezes and turns into ice, it takes up nearly ⅒ as much space again, and so it exerts pressure, widening the cracks until they split apart.

➤ HOW ARE LIMESTONE CAVES FORMED?

Rainwater slowly dissolves limestone, opening up cracks in the surface and wearing out holes. Over time, the holes eventually lead down into huge caves.

➤ CAN PLANTS CHANGE THE LAND?

Plant roots can break up rock. When the seed of a tree falls into a crack in a rock, it grows roots that push downward. As the roots grow, they push against the sides of the crack until the rock splits apart.

WHAT IS A SPELUNKER?

Pitches or shafts are holes in the ground where people called spelunkers (below) can climb down to explore limestone caves. They are formed when the roofs of shallow caves collapse.

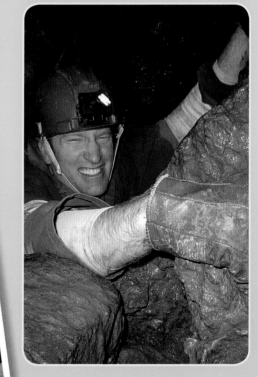

TREE ROOTS

Tree roots grow into cracks in the rock, forcing it to split apart.

The work of rivers >

Rivers erode, or wear away, the land. Young rivers push loose rocks down steep slopes. The rocks rub against riverbeds and deepen valleys. The rocks also rub against each other and break into finer pieces.

> WHERE DO RIVERS START?

Some rivers start at springs, where groundwater reaches the surface. Others start at the ends of melting glaciers or are the outlets of lakes. Tributary rivers are rivers that flow into a main river. For example, the River Amazon's many tributaries include the rivers Negro, Santiago, and Javari. Tributaries swell the amount of water in the main river and increase its load of worn material.

> WHAT IS AN OXBOW LAKE?

In old age, rivers flow more slowly. Sometimes they change course. Cut-off bends become oxbow lakes, with a distinctive curved shape.

CANYON

Young rivers flow swiftly and can wear out deep gorges.

NILE DELTA

As it meets the sea, the river moves slowly across flat plains.

WHAT ARE DELTAS?

Deltas are areas of sediments, made up of sand, mud, and silt, that pile up around the mouths of some rivers. In many rivers, currents sweep the sediments into the sea.

HOW DO CANYONS FORM?

A fast-moving river, carrying with it large rocks, can slowly wear away the riverbed. Over time, the river may erode a steep canyon.

WHY DO WATERFALLS OCCUR?

Waterfalls can occur when rivers cross hard rocks. When softer rocks downstream are worn away, the hard rocks form a ledge over which the river plunges in a waterfall.

IGUAZÚ FALLS

On the border of Brazil and Argentina, the falls are up to 270 feet high.

The Work of seas →

Waves continually batter the shore. Large waves pick up sand and pebbles, and hurl them at cliffs. This can hollow out the bottom layers of the cliff until the top collapses. Waves and tides can also move beach sand and gravel.

› WHAT ARE SPITS?

Waves and currents transport sand, gravel, and pebbles along coasts. In places where the coasts change direction, the worn sand and pebbles pile up in narrow ridges called spits.

› DOES THE SEA WEAR AWAY THE LAND?

Waves wear away soft rocks to form bays, while harder rocks on either side form capes. Parts of the coast of northeast England have been worn back by 3 miles in the last 2,000 years.

› WHAT IS A BAYMOUTH BAR?

Some spits join one cape to another. They are called baymouth bars because they can cut off bays from the sea, turning them into enclosed lagoons.

BEACH GROINS

Groins are built at many beach resorts to prevent the continual movement of sand by sea currents.

❯ WHAT IS A BLOWHOLE?

It is a hole in the rock formed above a sea cave. When waves enter the mouth of the cave, they are funneled up into the blowhole, sometimes causing spectacular blasts of water.

ARCHES AND STACKS

Waves hollow out arches (above) in rocky capes, which eventually collapse into stacks (below).

TOP ? QUESTION

WHAT ARE ARCHES AND STACKS?

Waves attack capes from both sides, wearing away caves in the cliffs. Eventually a natural arch is formed when two caves meet. When the arch collapses, all that remains is an isolated rock, called a stack.

❯ HOW CAN PEOPLE SLOW DOWN WAVE EROSION?

On many beaches, structures are built at right angles to the shore. These groins slow down the movement of sand by waves and currents.

The work of ice >

A glacier is a slow-moving river of ice. Glaciers form in cold mountain areas, when snow compacts into ice. Eventually the ice starts to move downhill. Rocks frozen into the glaciers erode the valleys through which they flow.

> WHAT IS MORAINE?

Ice from mountain tops spills downhill to form glaciers. These carry worn rock, called moraine.

MORAINE RIDGES

Dark ridges of moraine can be seen in this glacier in Switzerland.

> WHAT IS A GLACIAL LAKE?

A melting glacier often leaves behind large patches of ice in hollows along its path. These will eventually melt to create lakes.

> WHICH IS THE LARGEST GLACIER?

The Lambert Glacier in Antarctica is the world's largest. It is 300 miles long.

GLACIAL LAKES

As it melted, the glacier left behind deposits of ice in hollows. The ice melted to form a series of lakes.

HOW CAN WE TELL THAT AN AREA WAS ONCE COVERED BY ICE?

Certain features give this away. Mountain areas contain steep valleys worn by glaciers. Armchair-shape basins where glacier ice formed are called cirques. Knife-edge ridges between cirques are called arêtes. Peaks called horns were carved when three or more cirques formed back to back.

GLACIAL VALLEY

Ice-worn valleys are U shape, with steep sides and flat bottoms.

IS GLOBAL WARMING MAKING THE GLACIERS MELT?

Rising temperatures are making glaciers shrink and disappear all over the world. Some glaciers are retreating at a rate of 50 feet every year.

WHAT ARE ERRATICS?

Erratics are boulders made out of a rock that is different from the rocks on which they rest. They were carried there by moving ice.

CIRQUE

A cirque is an armchair-shape basin eroded at a glacier's head.

Ice ages >

During ice ages, temperatures fall and ice sheets spread over large areas. Several ice ages have occurred in the earth's history, dramatically shaping our planet.

WHEN WAS THE LAST ICE AGE?

The last ice age began about 1.6 million years ago and ended 10,000 years ago. The ice age included warm periods and long periods of bitter cold.

WHAT ARE FJORDS?

Fiords are deep, water-filled valleys that wind inland along coasts. They were once river valleys that were deepened by glaciers during the last ice age.

NORWEGIAN FJORD

Fjords were formed by glacial erosion (see pp. 122–123) and may be as much as 4,300 feet deep.

❯ HOW MUCH OF THE WORLD IS COVERED BY ICE?

Ice covers about 10 percent of the world's land. But during the last ice age, it spread over much of northern North America and Europe. The same ice sheet reached what are now New York City and London.

BEN BULBEN

This ridge in Ireland, called Ben Bulben, was cut by glaciers in the last ice age.

❯ DO ICE AGES CHANGE THE LANDSCAPE?

Yes! North America and Northern Europe are marked by glacial valleys, fjords, and erratics.

WHAT ARE THE WORLD'S LARGEST BODIES OF ICE TODAY?

The largest bodies of ice are the ice sheets of Antarctica and Greenland. Smaller ice caps occur in the Arctic, while mountain glaciers are found around the world.

ICE SHEET

Although we are in an interglacial period, ice still covers our poles.

Changing deserts

In deserts, wind-blown sand is important in shaping the scenery. It acts like the sandblasters that are used to clean dirty city buildings. It polishes rocks, hollows out caves in cliffs, and shapes boulders.

TOP ? QUESTION

WHAT ARE DUST STORMS?

Desert winds sweep fine dust high into the air during choking dust storms. Wind from the Sahara in North Africa is often blown across southern Europe, carrying the pinkish dust with it.

> CAN WATER CHANGE DESERT SCENERY?

Thousands of years ago, many deserts were rainy areas, and many land features were shaped by rivers. Flash floods sometimes occur in deserts. They sweep away a lot of worn material.

> WHAT IS A MUSHROOM ROCK?

In the desert, winds lift grains of sand, which are then blown and bounced forward. Sand grains are heavy and seldom rise over 6 feet above ground level. Boulders whose bases have been worn by wind-blown sand are top-heavy and mushroom shape.

BARCHAN DUNE

Tall barchan dunes form in sandy deserts where the wind direction is constant.

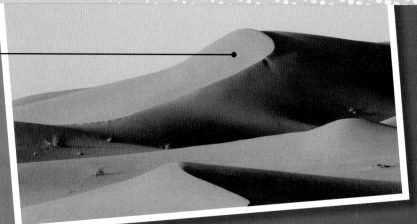

HOW ARE SAND DUNES FORMED?

The wind blowing across a desert piles the sand up in hills called dunes. Where the wind directions keep changing, the dunes have no particular shape. But when they blow mainly from one direction, crescent-shape dunes called barchans form. Barchans may occur singly or in clusters.

WHAT IS A WADI?

Wadis are dry waterways in deserts. Travelers sometimes shelter in them at night. But a freak storm can quickly fill them with water and drowning can be a real danger.

MUSHROOM ROCK

The Western Desert in Egypt is the home of dramatic mushroom rocks.

Changing Poles >

The North Pole lies in the middle of the Arctic Ocean, which is covered by sea ice for much of the year. The South Pole lies in the freezing continent of Antarctica, which is covered by the world's largest ice sheet.

ICEBERG

Penguins cluster on an iceberg off the coast of Antarctica.

> IS THE POLAR ICE MELTING?

Yes. Climate change is raising global temperatures, which is affecting the polar ice sheets and sea ice. By 2040, the Arctic Ocean may be free from sea ice in the summer, while ice shelves in northern Antarctica are collapsing.

> WHY ARE ICEBERGS DANGEROUS?

Icebergs are huge chunks of ice that naturally break off from glaciers. They float in the sea with nine-tenths of their bulk submerged, which makes them very dangerous to shipping. Icebergs from Greenland have sunk ships off the coast of North America.

ICE SHELF

Global warming has caused the collapse of 6,800 square miles of Antarctic ice shelf in the last 30 years.

> WHAT ARE ICE SHELVES?

Ice shelves are large blocks of ice joined to Antarctica's ice sheet, but which jut out over the sea. When chunks break away, they form flat, table top icebergs. Some of them are huge. One covered an area about the size of Belgium.

TOP QUESTION

WHAT IS IT LIKE AROUND THE NORTH POLE?

It is bitterly cold. The ice-covered Arctic Ocean is surrounded by northern North America, Asia, and Europe. In springtime, the sea ice is about 10 feet thick in mid-ocean. The ocean contains several islands, including Greenland.

> HOW THICK IS THE ICE IN ANTARCTICA?

Ice and snow cover 98 percent of Antarctica, with some coastal areas and high peaks being ice-free. The Antarctic ice sheet is the world's largest, and contains about seven-tenths of the world's freshwater. In places, the ice is up to 3 miles thick. The world's record lowest temperature, -199.48°F, was recorded at the Vostok research station in 1983.

> IS ANTARCTICA'S ICE SHEET GETTING THINNER?

Unfortunately, parts of the ice sheet are thinning. In West Antarctica, rising temperatures are thinning the ice by 3 feet per year.

People changing the earth >

Since humankind first learned to cut down trees to clear land for growing crops, we have changed the face of the earth. Today, some of these changes are threatening our environment, our health, and our future.

> WHAT IS AIR POLLUTION?

Air pollution occurs when gases, such as carbon dioxide, are emitted into the air by factories, homes, and offices. Vehicles also cause air pollution, which produces city smogs, acid rain, and global warming.

> WHAT IS HAPPENING TO THE WORLD'S FORESTS?

When trees are cut down without new trees being planted, deforestation takes place. Today, the tropical rain forests are particularly affected by deforestation. These forests contain more than half of the world's species—many are threatened with extinction.

DEFORESTATION

Around 32 million acres of forest are lost each year.

› WHAT IS DESERTIFICATION?

Human misuse of the land near deserts, caused by cutting down trees and overgrazing grasslands, may turn fertile land into desert. This is called desertification. Natural climate changes may also create deserts. This happened in the Sahara about 7,000 years ago.

› WHAT IS GLOBAL WARMING?

It is a rise in average worldwide temperatures. This is partly caused by human activities, such as deforestation and the burning of fossil fuels, such as coal. These activities release greenhouse gases, such as the carbon dioxide stored in trees. These gases trap heat in the earth's atmosphere. Global warming will probably cause changes in rainfall patterns, causing floods in some areas and droughts in others.

THE MALDIVES

The Maldives is a chain of coral islands that is threatened by rising sea levels.

› WILL GLOBAL WARMING AFFECT ANY ISLAND NATIONS?

Coral islands are low-lying. If global warming melts the world's ice, then sea levels will rise. Some countries such as the Maldives and Kiribati, could vanish under the waves.

CITY SMOG

Smog causes an increase in asthma and allergies. It is dangerous for people with heart and lung problems.

The human touch ➤

The environment is in a delicate balance. Industry, farming, and the growth of cities can destroy that balance. But not all human change is harmful, with deserts and sea being turned into farmland.

➤ WHAT IS THREATENING FISH IN THE SEA?

Coral reefs and mangrove swamps are breeding places for many fishes. The destruction or pollution of these areas is threatening the numbers of fish in the oceans.

➤ CAN THE POLLUTION OF RIVERS HARM PEOPLE?

When factories pump poisonous wastes into rivers, creatures living near the rivers' mouths, such as shellfish, absorb poison into their bodies. When people eat such creatures, they, too, are poisoned.

RIVER POLLUTION

Water pollution is a major cause of death and disease. Pollution includes garbage, chemicals, and sewage.

HOW HAVE PEOPLE TURNED SEA INTO LAND?

People sometimes turn useless coastal land into fertile farmland. The Netherlands is a flat country and about two-fifths of it is below sea level at high tide. The Dutch have created new land by building dykes called polders (sea walls, seen below) around areas once under the sea. Rainwater washes the salt from the soil and the polder land finally becomes fertile.

> CAN DESERTS BE FARMED?

In the United States and other countries, barren deserts have been turned into farmland by irrigation. The land is watered from wells that tap groundwater, or the water is piped from faraway areas.

IRRIGATION

Circles of irrigated land can be seen in the desert of the southwestern United States.

> WHAT IS SOIL EROSION?

Natural erosion, caused by running water, winds, and other forces, is a slow process. Soil erosion occurs when people cut down trees and farm the land. Soil erosion on land made bare by people is a much faster process than natural erosion.

> WHAT IS A DAM?

A dam is a man-made barrier that holds back flowing water. Dams are often built to retain water in order to generate hydroelectric power or for irrigation. The construction of a dam can sometimes place large areas under water.

Natural Wonders

The world's natural wonders can be found on every continent. Many of these beautiful features were created by weathering, erosion, and the work of rivers, seas, and ice.

> HOW ARE NATURAL WONDERS PROTECTED?

One important step in protecting natural wonders was made in 1872, when the world's first national park was founded at Yellowstone in Wyoming. Since then, national parks have been founded around the world.

GRAND CANYON

The Grand Canyon is regarded as one of the greatest natural wonders.

> WHICH IS THE WORLD'S LARGEST CANYON?

Most lists of natural wonders include the Grand Canyon. It is the world's largest canyon and the most awe-inspiring. The canyon is 276 miles long and about a mile deep. It was worn down by the Colorado River over the last 6 million years.

AYERS ROCK

Ayers Rock in Australia is an "island mountain," an immense rock left over after the erosion of a mountain.

> WHAT IS THE GREAT PEBBLE?

"Uluru" is an Australian Aboriginal word meaning "great pebble." Also called Ayers Rock, Uluru is the world's biggest monolith (single rock) and lies in central Australia.

> IS THERE A LAKE UNDER ANTARCTICA?

Scientists have found a lake, around the size of Lake Ontario in North America, hidden under Antarctica. It may contain creatures that lived on the earth millions of years ago.

TOP QUESTION ?

WHERE IS THE MATTERHORN?

The Matterhorn is a magnificent mountain on Switzerland's border with Italy. It was created by glaciers wearing away the mountain from opposite sides.

MATTERHORN

The Matterhorn reaches a height of 14,700 feet above sea level.

More natural wonders

Many locations may compete for the fame of being the longest beach or the tallest stalagmite. What we do know for certain is that our natural wonders must be protected for future generations.

MOUNT FUJI

Women were forbidden to ascend Mount Fuji until the eighteenth century.

WHERE IS THE WORLD'S TALLEST STALAGMITE?

Many stalagmites claim this honor. The winner may be a 220-feet-tall stalagmite in the cave of San Martin Infierno in Cuba.

WHICH IS THE LONGEST BEACH?

At 78 miles long, Cox's Bazar Beach in Bangladesh is the longest sandy sea beach. The beach is used by both fishermen and swimmers.

WHERE ARE THE NEEDLES?

The Needles are a row of chalk stacks, eroded by waves, that lie off the Isle of Wight in southern England.

WHICH JAPANESE WONDER ATTRACTS PILGRIMS?

Mount Fuji in Japan is a beautiful volcanic cone. Many people regard it as a sacred mountain—a dwelling place for the gods—and they make long pilgrimages to the top.

TOP QUESTION ?

WHERE IS "SMOKE THAT THUNDERS"?

The local name of the beautiful Victoria Falls on the Zambezi River between Zambia and Zimbabwe is Mosi-oa-Tunya, meaning "smoke that thunders." The falls are 355 feet tall in some places.

WHAT IS THE GREAT BARRIER REEF?

The Great Barrier Reef is the world's longest group of coral reefs and islands. It lies off the northeast coast of Australia and is about 1,250 miles long.

GREAT BARRIER REEF

The reef is made of billions of tiny organisms, known as coral polyps. It supports a wide variety of wildlife.

Plants

Growing in the sun ➤

GREEN LEAVES

Plants reduce carbon dioxide and produce vital oxygen through photosynthesis.

There are 287,655 named species of plants, although many more are believed to exist. These range from trees, bushes, and herbs to grasses, ferns, and mosses. Most plants get their energy for growing from sunlight, using a process called photosynthesis.

➤ HOW DO GREEN PLANTS FEED?

Green plants make their own food in a process called photosynthesis. Chlorophyll helps to trap energy from the sun. Plants use this energy to convert water and carbon dioxide into sugars and starch.

➤ WHY ARE MOST PLANTS GREEN?

Most plants are green because they contain the green pigment chlorophyll in their stems and leaves. Sometimes the green pigment is masked by other colors, such as red. This means that not all plants that contain chlorophyll look green.

→ HOW DOES A FLOWER FORM SO QUICKLY?

When a flower opens out from a bud, it may appear in just a few hours. This is possible because the flower is already formed in miniature inside the bud, just waiting to open out. The bud opens as its cells take in water and grow.

BLOSSOMING

Buds open in the warm and sunny weather of spring.

→ HOW MUCH SUGAR DOES PHOTOSYNTHESIS MAKE IN A YEAR?

Plants turn the sugar they make by photosynthesis into other chemical compounds that they need for growth and development. They also use sugar to make energy. Some scientists have estimated that the total mass of green plants alive in the entire world makes more than 190 billion tons of sugar every year by photosynthesis.

→ WHAT MAKES A SEED GROW?

To grow, a seed needs moisture, warmth, and air. Some seeds can only germinate (begin to grow) if they have first been in the low temperatures of winter. The seeds of some plants can lie dormant (inactive) for years before germinating.

WHY DO SHOOTS GROW UPWARD?

Most shoots grow upward, toward the sunlight. The growing tip of the shoot can detect the direction of the light, and chemicals are released that make it grow more on the lower or darker side, thus turning the shoot upward.

SHOOTING UP

Like most plants, a bean shoot relies on the soil for water and support.

Feeding ›

Plants need water, mineral salts, and foods, such as carbohydrates, in order to grow. Green plants make their own foods, while other plants may take in food from decaying plants or animals, or directly from other living plants.

› HOW DOES A VENUS FLYTRAP CATCH ITS PREY?

The flytrap is a carnivorous (meat-eating) plant that catches insects and other small animals. The trap is a flattened, hinged pad at the end of each leaf, fringed with bristles. When an insect lands on the pad and touches one of the sensitive hairs growing there, the trap is sprung and closes over the insect.

› HOW DOES A PARASITIC PLANT FEED?

Parasitic plants do not need to make their own food, and many are not green. Instead, they grow into the tissues of another plant, called the host, and tap into its food and water transportation system, taking all the nourishment they need.

ROOTS

Roots anchor the plant while taking in water and mineral salts.

TOP ? QUESTION

WHY DO ROOTS GROW DOWNWARD?

Roots grow down because the root responds to gravity by releasing chemicals that prevent growth on the lower side, thus turning the root downward.

› HOW DOES MISTLETOE FEED?

Mistletoe is a hemi-parasitic plant, which means that it takes some of its nutrients from a host plant and some from its own photosynthesis. It can attach itself to the branches of many different trees and shrubs.

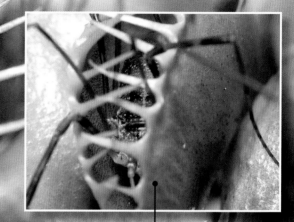

PREY

A struggling insect is caught in the plant's hinged trap.

VENUS FLY-TRAP

The trap's hinges can snap shut in just ¹/₁₀ seconds.

➤ HOW DO PLANTS TAKE IN WATER?

Plants use their extensive root systems to take in water from the ground. Each root branches into a network of rootlets, which in turn bear root hairs. Water passes into the root across the cell walls of millions of tiny root hairs.

➤ HOW FAST DOES SAP FLOW THROUGH A TREE?

Sap is the fluid that transports water and food through plants. Sap may flow through a tree as fast as 3 feet every hour.

Reproduction

Many plants reproduce by pollination. The pollen, containing the male cells, fertilizes the female ovules, which then produce seeds. The pollen can be taken to its destination by insects, birds, the wind, or water.

WHAT HAPPENS IN A FLOWER AFTER POLLINATION?

After pollination, the pollen that has landed on the stigma of another flower of the same species will begin to germinate if conditions are right. It sends a tube down into the ovary of the flower, which it enters to fertilize an ovule. Each ovule can now become a seed.

WHICH FLOWERS LAST FOR JUST ONE DAY?

The flowers of morning glory and daylilies open each morning and shrivel and die toward evening.

MORNING GLORY

The flowers are pollinated by bees, hummingbirds, butterflies, and moths.

CAN PLANTS REPRODUCE WITHOUT SEEDS?

Some plants, such as mosses, liverworts, and ferns, do not produce seeds. Instead, they spread by dispersing spores, which can produce a new plant without the need of pollination. Other plants can reproduce by growing runners or splitting off from bulbs, or swollen stems.

TOP QUESTION ?

HOW ARE FLOWERS POLLINATED?

Many flowers have evolved their colors and scent to attract insects. The animal lands on the flower, gets showered with pollen, then moves to the next flower, transporting the pollen.

SOWING SEEDS

Seeds must be dispersed, or spread around, so that some will find suitable places to germinate. Seeds contained in berries and fruit are spread in bird droppings.

POLLINATION

Bees, wasps, and butterflies like to feed from flowers' nectar.

❯ WHICH FLOWERS ARE POLLINATED BY MAMMALS?

The flowers of the African baobab tree are pollinated by bushbabies and bats.

❯ HOW ARE SEEDS DISPERSED?

Many seeds are dispersed by animals. Birds eat berries and pass out the tougher seeds unharmed in their droppings. Some fruit capsules have hooks that catch in animal fur and are transported that way. Many seeds can be carried by the wind. The sycamore has "helicopter" wings to carry it along.

Plants and the environment >

Plants are vital to the environment. In fact, without plants, there would be no life on our planet. Plants are key producers of oxygen, which most animals need to survive. Many animals, including humans, rely on plants for shelter, water, food, and oxygen.

CATERPILLAR

A tree's leaves may provide food for caterpillars.

WHAT IS THE NITROGEN CYCLE?

Bacteria in the soil use nitrogen from the air and turn it into a form that plants can use. Plants then use the nitrogen in their cells to make complex compounds, such as proteins. When animals eat plants, the nitrogen returns to the soil in their droppings. It also returns when plant and animal bodies decay and rot.

HOW DO PLANTS RECYCLE WATER?

Plants help to return water to the air through the process of transpiration. This is when water evaporates from the stems and leaves of plants. Water enters the plant through its roots. A column of water moves up through the plant, from the roots all the way through the trunk or stem, into the leaves.

TOP QUESTION

WHAT LIVES IN A TREE?

Many species of beetles lay their eggs in a tree's bark. Birds select a fork in a branch to build a nest, or use a natural hole in the trunk, and wild bees may also choose to nest inside a hollow tree. Many mammals are tree dwellers, including squirrels, monkeys, sloths, bats, and koalas.

› HOW ARE PLANTS USED TO CLEAN UP SEWAGE?

Sewage treatment plants use tiny algae and other microscopic organisms in their filter beds. These algae and other organisms feed on the pollutants in the water and help to make it clean.

HERBIVORE

Caterpillars are the larvae of moths and butterflies. They only eat plant matter.

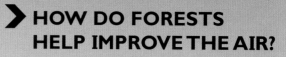

› HOW DO FORESTS HELP IMPROVE THE AIR?

Forests do this by releasing huge quantities of water vapor and oxygen into the atmosphere. Plants also absorb carbon dioxide, and help prevent this gas from building up to damaging levels.

Plants and the soil >

Plants take water and nutrients from the soil, only to return them in a never-ending, finely balanced cycle. But this cycle can be destroyed by humans if we forget to care for our vital forests and fields.

WHAT HAPPENS TO ALL THE LEAVES THAT FALL?

Huge quantities of leaves fall from forest trees, but they do not build up on the woodland floor from year to year. The dead leaves are attacked, for example by fungi and bacteria, and break down, becoming part of the soil. The leaves are also eaten by animals, including worms and insects.

HOW DO PLANTS MAKE SOIL MORE FERTILE?

When plants die, they decompose, releasing the chemicals in their tissues into the surrounding soil. The mixture of rotting leaves and other plant material in the soil is called humus, and this makes the soil more fertile.

LEAF FOOD

Fallen leaves provide food for animals and fertilize the soil.

➤ WHAT IS OVERGRAZING?

It is when livestock, such as cows and sheep, are allowed to eat the grasses and other plants in one area for too long. The plants are not able to recover and, in dry areas, the land may become eroded or turn into desert.

➤ HOW DO PLANTS COLONIZE BARE GROUND?

Some plants can quickly colonize bare soil by germinating rapidly from lightweight, wind-blown seeds. Some colonizing plants spread by growing runners, which split off, becoming new plants.

HOW DO PLANTS HELP US RECLAIM LAND?

Several types of grass, including marram, can be planted on coastal dunes. Their roots anchor the sand and help to stop it from blowing away. Plants can even begin to reclaim land contaminated by industrial poisons. Some species have evolved forms that can tolerate toxic substances. They gradually improve the fertility and build up the soil so that other plants can grow there, too.

DANDELION

A dandelion's seeds are carried by "parachutes" to take root on bare ground.

➤ HOW CAN PLANTS BE USED TO HELP STOP EROSION?

Erosion is when soil is loosened and removed by the action of natural force, such as wind and water. This can often be reduced or prevented by using plants. The roots of the plants trap the loose soil and stop it from being blown away. This can be useful on steep slopes or the edges of deserts.

Plants as food

About 12,000 species of plants are known to have been used as food by people, and about 150 of these are in regular cultivation. Human cultivation of plants is part of agriculture, along with raising animals. Without agriculture, there would be no human civilization.

> WHAT ARE THE MOST IMPORTANT FOOD CROPS?

The most important crops are the cereals, such as wheat, rice, and corn (maize). These form the basis of many people's diet. Tuber crops, such as potatoes, are also widely grown. All these foods provide carbohydrates, while legumes, such as peas, beans, and lentils, are rich in protein.

PEACHES

Peaches grow well in warm climates such as, the Mediterranean and the southern United States.

> WHICH FRUIT IS GROWN FOR FOOD?

Fruit of the temperate regions include apples, pears, and strawberries. In warmer regions, there is citrus fruits, such as oranges and lemons, and other fruit, such as papayas, pineapples, and melons. Some fruit has a savory flavor, such as avocados and bell peppers.

SUGAR MAPLE

Maple syrup is often used as a sweetener with pancakes.

➤ WHAT TREES GIVE US A SWEET, SUGARY SYRUP?

The sugar maple has a sweet sap, which is harvested to make maple syrup. Most maple syrup comes from the province of Quebec, in Canada.

➤ WHAT IS THE AMAZON COW-TREE?

The Amazon cow-tree is a tropical fig. It takes its name from the fact that it produces a milk-like sap, or latex, which can be drunk just like cow's milk.

SUNFLOWER

Sunflower oil is commonly used for frying food and contains essential vitamin E.

➤ WHICH PLANTS GIVE US OIL?

The seeds of many plants are rich in oil, which they store as a source of food and energy. We extract oil from several of these plants, including olives, sunflowers, corn (maize), soy beans, peanuts, rapeseed, sesame, and African oil palm.

➤ WHAT PLANTS ARE USED TO MAKE SUGAR?

The main source of sugar is the sweet stems of sugar cane, a tall grass that grows in tropical countries. In some temperate areas, including Europe, there are large crops of sugar beet. This plant stores sugar in its thickened roots. In some parts of the tropics, the sap of the sugar palm is made into sugar.

Harvesting the land →

It is not just our staple crops, such as cereals and potatoes, that are provided by plants. Drinks, such as tea, coffee, wine, and beer, are made from plants. Sometimes we do not even notice the plants on our plate, such as the pectin from plant cells that stiffens gelatin.

❯ WHAT IS BREADFRUIT?

Breadfruit is a tree native to the Malay Archipelego. It grows to about 65 feet and has large edible fruit, which is eaten as a vegetable. The related jackfruit, from India and Malaysia, also has edible fruits up to 24 inches long.

TOP QUESTION?

HOW IS TEA MADE?

Tea comes from the leaves of a camellia grown on hillsides in India, Sri Lanka, Indonesia, Japan, and China. The young leaf tips are harvested, dried, and then crushed to make tea.

EAR OF WHEAT

Wheat is used to make flour for bread, cookies, cakes, pasta, noodles, and couscous.

❯ WHERE DID WHEAT COME FROM?

Wheat is one of the oldest known crops. It was probably first cultivated over 6,000 years ago in Mesopotamia (present-day Iraq). Many useful crop plants have their origins in the Middle East. Other examples are barley, oats and rye, peas and lentils, onions, olives, figs, apples, and pears.

TEA PICKING

After water, tea is the world's most consumed drink.

❯ HOW IS CHOCOLATE MADE?

The cacao tree comes originally from the lowland rain forests of the Amazon and Orinoco. The fruit, called pods, develops on the sides of the trunk, and each pod contains about 20 to 60 seeds—the cocoa "beans". The beans must be fermented, roasted, and ground before they become cocoa powder, the raw material for making chocolate.

❯ WHERE DOES COFFEE COME FROM?

The coffee plant is a large shrub, and its berries are used to make coffee. The ripe berries are harvested, then dried to remove the flesh from the hard pits inside. These are the coffee "beans", which are then often roasted.

❯ WHERE WERE POTATOES FIRST GROWN?

Potatoes grow wild in the Andes Mountains of South America and were first gathered as food by the native people of that region. All the many varieties grown today derive from that wild source.

COCOA POD

Today, cocoa is a highly valuable crop in west Africa and the Caribbean.

Plants as medicine >

ROSY PERIWINKLE

Extracts from this plant, vinblastine and vincristine, are used by many international drug companies.

Plants have been used as medicine for at least 100,000 years. In much of the world, especially in China and India, herbal remedies are used more than any other kind of medicine. Today, scientists are still researching the valuable healing properties of plants for use in conventional medicines.

> CAN PLANTS HELP FIGHT CANCER?

Several plants are effective against cancer tumors. One of the most famous is the rosy periwinkle. One of its extracts, vincristine, is very effective against some types of leukemia, a cancer of the blood.

> WHICH PLANTS AID DIGESTION?

Many plants, including the herbs and spices used in cooking, help digestion. In Europe, the bitter extract of wild gentians provides a good remedy for digestive problems.

WHAT IS GINSENG?

Ginseng is a plant related to ivy, and has been used in herbal medicine for centuries. It is claimed—but not proved—to help many conditions, including fatigue and depression, kidney disease, heart problems, and headaches.

WHICH PLANT HELPS COMBAT MALARIA?

Quinine, from the bark of the quinine tree, which grows in the South American Andes, can cure or prevent malaria. Before the widespread use of quinine, malaria used to kill 2 million people each year.

GINSENG

Ginseng root is often taken in dried form.

WHICH PLANT IS BELIEVED TO HELP ASTHMA?

Lungwort is a herb with purple flowers and spotted leaves that are said to look like lungs. For this reason, it is sometimes used to treat asthma. There is no definite proof that it works.

LUNGWORT

The lungwort herb gets its name from the belief that it helps the lungs.

CAN WILLOWS HELP PAIN?

Willow twigs were once chewed to give pain relief. A compound similar to the drug aspirin was once extracted from willows and the herb meadowsweet, known as spiraea—giving aspirin its name.

Materials from plants >

Plant materials are an essential part of our lives, keeping us warm, dry, safe, and even—in the case of musical instruments—entertained. From wood to leaves, plants supply many of our raw materials.

> WHAT TYPES OF THINGS CAN BE MADE FROM PLANTS?

We make all kinds of things from plant materials. Wood alone is used to make countless objects, big and small, from construction lumber to toys. All kinds of cloth are also made from plants—and so is the paper you are looking at!

TOP QUESTION ?

HOW MANY THINGS CAN BE MADE FROM BAMBOO?

Bamboo is one of the world's most useful plant products. It is used for scaffolding and building houses, and for making paper, furniture, pipes, canes, and (when split) for mats, hats, umbrellas, baskets, blinds, fans, and brushes. Some bamboos have young shoots that are delicious to eat.

> WHAT IS JOJOBA?

Jojoba is a bush found in Mexico. The fruits have a high-grade oily wax. It is used as a lubricant, in printing inks, and in body lotions and shampoo.

> WHAT ARE VIOLINS MADE OF?

The body of a violin is usually made from finely carved spruce and maple woods, creating its beautiful sound.

THATCHED COTTAGE

Traditional English cottages have a wood frame and roofs of thatched straw.

> ## WHAT IS BALSA?

Balsa is the world's lightest wood—it floats high in water. Balsa trees grow in tropical South America. Balsa wood is used for making models, such as airplanes, and also for rafts, life preservers, and insulation.

> ## WHAT IS RAFFIA?

Raffia is a natural fiber made from the young leaves of the raffia palm, which grows in tropical Africa. Raffia is used in handicrafts, such as basketry.

RAFFIA BAGS

Dyeing and weaving raffia is a traditional handicraft.

BAMBOO CAFÉ

Giant bamboo plants shade bamboo furniture in China.

Plant products →

Plant products are chosen for different uses, depending on their natural properties. The softness of cotton makes it ideal for clothing. The springiness of rubber makes it perfect for products from rubber bands to rubber gloves.

› HOW IS CORK PRODUCED?

Cork comes from a tree called the cork oak. The cork is the thick, spongy bark. It is stripped away from the lower trunk, then left to grow back for up to 10 years before the next harvest. Cork is used to make many things, from bottle corks and bulletin boards to floor tiles.

CORK OAK

Cork oaks grow wild around the Mediterranean Sea and have been cultivated in Portugal and Spain.

› WHAT IS KAPOK?

Kapok is similar to cotton. It comes from the kapok tree, which is cultivated in Asia and can be as tall as 160 feet. The fluffy seed fibers are used to stuff mattresses, jackets, quilts, and sleeping bags.

COTTON

Cotton plants grow in the Americas, India, and Africa.

> HOW IS COTTON TURNED INTO CLOTH?

Cotton is a soft fiber that grows naturally around the seeds of the cotton plant, forming "bolls." These are "ginned" to remove the seeds; spun, or twisted, into thread; and then woven to make cloth.

> WHAT IS RUBBER?

Rubber is the sap of some plants, particularly the para rubber tree. The trees are pierced, or tapped, and the sap drips slowly into a waiting container.

> WHAT WOOD MAKES THE BEST CRICKET BAT?

The best bats are made in India, from the wood of the cricket bat willow, a white willow. The blade (the part the ball strikes) is made from willow, and the handle from a different wood or cane.

WILLOW BAT

Willow is lightweight but will not splinter when hit by a ball.

> CAN PLANTS PRODUCE FUEL TO RUN CARS?

The copaiba tree of the Amazon rain forest yields an oil similar to diesel fuel that can be used to run engines. Oilseed rape, soybean, and the petroleum nut tree of Southeast Asia can also be used to produce biofuels, or plant fuels. As crude oil reserves are used up, biofuels may become more important.

Extreme plants ❯

The many species of plants are all competing for resources. They have evolved countless extreme survival strategies, from great height to immense roots. They have adapted to hostile environments, from deserts to mountains, so that they can find a place to grow and thrive.

❯ WHICH IS THE LARGEST SEED?

The coco de mer of the Seychelles has the largest seeds, each weighing up to 48 pounds. They are produced inside a big fruit that takes six years to grow.

❯ WHAT IS THE SMALLEST FLOWERING PLANT?

A tiny tropical floating duckweed is the world's smallest flowering plant. Some species measure less than one-fiftieth of an inch across, even when full grown.

DUCKWEED

These simple plants just consist of a platelike structure that floats on the water surface.

BANYAN TREE

This single banyan looks as if it is a whole grove of trees.

The oldest known plant may be the creosote bush. It grows in the southwestern United States and in Mexico. Some of these bushes are thought to be 11,700 years old. The bristlecone pine, which grows mainly in the southwestern United States, notably in the White Mountains of California, is also extremely old. The oldest is about 4,900 years old.

❯ WHAT PLANT CAN SPREAD ACROSS THE WIDEST AREA?

The banyan of India and Pakistan often starts life as an epiphyte—a small plant growing on another tree. As it grows, it sends down woody roots that come to resemble tree trunks. Eventually it can seem like a grove of separate trees. One 200-year-old banyan had 100 "trunks."

OLD PINE

Although the original branches die, bristlecone pines can live for 5,000 years.

❯ WHICH PLANT HAS THE LONGEST LEAF?

The raffia palm of tropical Africa produces the longest known leaves. The stalk can be nearly 13 feet and the leaf blade over 65 feet long.

❯ HOW DEEP ARE THE DEEPEST ROOTS?

Roots of a South African fig were found to have penetrated 400 feet below the dry surface.

Plant records

Tall conifers tower above other plants in their forest, while giant flowers feed among roots on the ground. In the oceans and lakes, seaweeds and waterlilies grow huge to absorb nutrients and sunlight.

TOP QUESTION ?

WHAT IS THE LARGEST FLOWER?

It's the rafflesia, which grows in Southeast Asia. It is a parasite, growing on the stems of lianas in the forest. Flowers can measure 35 inches—and they stink, mimicking the aroma of rotting flesh to attract flies to pollinate the flower.

> WHICH PLANT GROWS THE SLOWEST?

The record for the slowest-growing plant probably goes to the dioon plant. The dioon grows in Mexico, and one specimen was recorded to have an average growth rate of one thirty-fifth of an inch per year.

> WHICH PLANT GROWS THE FASTEST?

The giant bamboo of Burma grows at up to 1 foot per day, making it one of the fastest growing of all plants. However, another species from India, the spiny bamboo, holds the record for growth in a greenhouse—it achieved 35 inches in a day.

❯ WHAT IS THE WORLD'S LONGEST SEAWEED?

Giant kelp is a huge seaweed that forms underwater forests in the coastal waters of California. Its fronds can be over 200 feet long, making it one of the tallest plants known.

GIANT KELP

Kelp forests are vital ecosystems that are home to many animals, from fish and starfish to sea urchins.

❯ WHICH IS THE TALLEST TREE?

The California redwood, which grows along the North American Pacific coast, is the tallest tree in the world, reaching 368 feet. Some Australian eucalyptus trees can grow to 300 feet.

❯ WHICH PLANT HAS THE LARGEST FLOATING LEAVES?

The giant water lily of the Amazon region has huge leaves. They grow up to almost 9 feet across, and can support the weight of a child.

GIANT WATER LILY

These lilies, which grow in still lakes and swamps, have stalks up to 23 feet long.

Life on the land

Rodents →

Rodents are mammals, which means they have backbones, they are hairy, and they produce milk to feed their young. Rodents are distinguished by having continuously growing incisor teeth. Squirrels, hamsters, beavers, rats, and mice are all rodents.

> WHY DO RODENTS HAVE LONG TEETH?

The two sharp teeth, called incisors, at the front of the rodent's jaw are the ones it uses for gnawing. A rodent's incisors get worn down as it gnaws tough food, but they keep on growing throughout its life.

NUTRIA TEETH

The nutria, which lives in wetlands, has huge, orange incisor teeth.

TOP ? QUESTION

WHY DO BEAVERS BUILD DAMS?

Beavers build their lodges, or homes, in streams or rivers. But first they need to build a dam to make an area of still water, or the current would wash the lodge away. With their huge front teeth, the beavers cut down trees to build the dam. They plaster the sides with mud and fill gaps with stones and sticks.

➤ WHICH IS THE BIGGEST RODENT?

The largest rodent in the world is the capybara, which lives in South America. It measures up to 4 feet long and weighs up to 140 pounds. One of the smallest rodents is the pygmy mouse of North America. It is only about 4 inches long, including its tail, and weighs just ¼ of an ounce.

CAPYBARA

The capybara lives in marshy places and feeds on grasses.

➤ WHEN IS A DOG REALLY A RAT?

A prairie dog is actually not a dog at all. It is a type of rodent, and lives in North America. Prairie dogs live in family groups of one adult male and several females and their young. A group of families makes a vast burrow of connecting chambers and tunnels called a colony.

➤ CAN FLYING SQUIRRELS REALLY FLY?

No, but they can glide from tree to tree. When the flying squirrel leaps into the air, it stretches out the skin flaps at the sides of its body, which act like a parachute, enabling it to glide gently between branches.

BEAVER LODGE

A beaver lodge is built of sticks behind a dam and has an underwater entrance.

Bears

There are eight species of bear. They range in size from the sun bear, which can weigh less than 110 pounds, to huge polar bears and brown bears. Bears have a large body, stocky legs, a long snout, shaggy hair, and sharp claws.

WHICH IS THE BIGGEST BEAR?

The polar bear of the Arctic is one of the largest bears. Full-grown males are up to 8 feet long. Polar bears are meat eaters and hunt seals, young walruses, and birds.

POLAR BEAR

The polar bear is the world's largest land-living predator.

CAN POLAR BEARS SWIM?

Polar bears swim well and spend long periods in the freezing Arctic water. They are well equipped to survive the cold. They have a dense layer of underfur as well as a thin layer of stiff, shiny outer coat. Under the skin is a thick layer of fat to give further protection.

HOW BIG IS A BABY BEAR?

Although adult bears are large, they have tiny babies. A huge polar bear, weighing more than several people, gives birth to cubs of only about 2 pounds, far smaller than most human babies. Baby pandas weigh as little as 3 ounces.

IS THE GIANT PANDA A BEAR?

For years, experts argued about whether this animal should be grouped with bears or raccoons or classed in a family of its own. Genetic evidence now suggests that the panda is a member of the bear family.

GIANT PANDA

Giant pandas live in bamboo forest reserves in west and central China.

> WHAT DO GIANT PANDAS EAT?

The main food of the giant panda is bamboo. An adult panda eats up to 40 pounds of bamboo leaves and stems a day.

TOP QUESTION ?

DO BEARS SLEEP THROUGH WINTER?

Brown bears (below), polar bears, and black bears that live in the far north sleep for much of the winter. Food supplies are poor, so the bears hide away in warm dens and live off their own fat reserves. Before their sleep, the bears eat as much food as they can.

TREE CLIMBER

Like all bears, giant pandas are excellent climbers. They often take shelter in hollow trees and rock crevices.

Wolves and dogs >

The canid family of mammals includes dogs, wolves, foxes, coyotes, dingoes, and jackals. Canids are meat eaters and have long legs for chasing their prey. Their sharp claws and teeth are perfect for slicing flesh.

HOW MANY KINDS OF DOG AND FOX ARE THERE?

There are about 35 species in the canid family, split between the "true dogs" and the "foxes." True dogs include wolves, jackals, and wild dogs.

DINGO

Dingoes hunt alone, returning to their pack every few days to socialize.

WHAT IS A DINGO?

Dingoes are Australian wild dogs. They are probably descended from dogs introduced 5,000–8,000 years ago by Aborigines. Nowadays, they hunt mainly sheep and rabbits. A fence of over 3,000 miles has been built across southeastern Australia to keep dingoes out of sheep-grazing land.

❯ WHAT DO FOXES EAT?

Foxes, such as the red fox, are hunting animals. They kill and eat small creatures, including rats, mice, and rabbits. But foxes are very adaptable and will eat more or less anything that comes their way, such as birds and birds' eggs, insects, and even fruit and berries. More and more foxes in cities are feasting on our discarded food from garbage cans and compost piles.

HOW BIG IS A WOLF PACK?

In areas where there are plenty of large animals to catch, a pack may contain up to 30 wolves. Hunting in a pack means that the wolves can kill prey much larger than themselves, such as moose. A wolf pack has a territory, which it defends against other wolves.

RED FOX PUP

Red fox pups are taken care of by their parents until they reach 8–10 months old.

❯ WHAT IS A COYOTE?

The coyote looks similar to a wolf, with large ears and long legs for running. It lives in North and Central America, where it hunts small mammals, such as squirrels and mice. Coyotes form a small pack but hunt with just one partner.

Cats

There are about 36 species of wild cat, ranging from the tiger to the African wild cat, which is closely related to the domestic cat. Wild cats live in every sort of habitat, from tropical rain forest to desert. There are no wild cats in Antarctica, Australia, or New Zealand.

> WHAT DO LIONS DO ALL DAY?

Like domestic cats, lions are actually asleep for a surprisingly large part of the day. As much as 20 hours a day are spent resting and grooming. The rest of the time is taken up with looking for prey, hunting, and feeding. Lionesses do most of the hunting, then share the catch with the rest of the pride.

TIGER

The pattern of stripes on a tiger's fur is unique. No two tigers have exactly the same pattern.

HUNTING LIONS

Lionesses develop a carefully coordinated group strategy to bring down their prey.

WHICH IS THE BIGGEST CAT?

Tigers are the biggest of the big cats. They can measure over 10 feet long, including the tail, and weigh 550 pounds or more. Tigers are becoming very rare. They live in parts of Asia, from snowy Siberia in the north to the tropical rain forests of Sumatra, Indonesia.

WHICH IS THE FASTEST CAT?

The cheetah is the fastest-running cat and one of the speediest of all animals over short distances. It has been timed running at more than 60 miles an hour over a distance of 600 feet—more than twice as fast as humans.

TOP QUESTION?

WHY DO TIGERS HAVE STRIPES?

A tiger's stripes help it hide among grasses and leaves so it can surprise its prey. Tigers cannot run fast for long distances, so they depend on being able to get close to their prey before making the final pounce. The stripes help to break up their outline and make them hard for prey to see.

SNOW LEOPARD

This big cat hunts alone, sometimes killing animals three times its size.

WHERE DO JAGUARS LIVE?

Jaguars live in the forests of Central and South America. The jaguar is a good climber and often clambers up a tree to watch for prey. It hunts other forest mammals, such as peccaries and capybaras, as well as birds and turtles.

WHAT IS A SNOW LEOPARD?

The snow leopard is a big cat that lives in the mountains of Central Asia. Its beautiful pale coat with dark markings has made it the target of fur poachers. Killing snow leopards for their fur is now illegal, but poaching still goes on.

Elephants >

Elephants are the largest land animals. There are probably three species: the African bush elephant, African forest elephant, and Asian elephant. Elephants have tusks, long trunks, flapping ears, and very thick skin.

> HOW LONG ARE AN ELEPHANT'S TUSKS?

An elephant's tusks grow throughout its life, so the oldest elephants have the longest tusks. One tusk in the British Museum in London measures 11 feet.

> WHY ARE BIG EARS USEFUL?

Elephants live in hot climates, so they flap their ears to create a breeze. This breeze cools their surface blood vessels, and the cooler blood is circulated to the rest of the elephant's body.

> HOW MUCH DO ELEPHANTS EAT?

A full-grown elephant eats 170 to 340 pounds of plant food a day. Its diet includes grass, twigs, branches, leaves, flowers, and fruits.

AFRICAN ELEPHANT

An elephant uses its tusks to dig for water, tree pulp, or roots, and to clear its path of trees and branches.

WHAT DO ELEPHANTS DO WITH THEIR TRUNKS?

Without its trunk, an elephant could not reach the ground to feed because its neck is so short. The trunk is also used for taking food from high in trees. The elephant can smell with its trunk, pick up objects, and caress its young. It drinks by sucking up water into its trunk and squirting it into its mouth. It also sprays itself with water or dust to clean its skin.

HOW BIG IS A BABY ELEPHANT?

A newborn African baby elephant weighs up to 260 pounds and stands over 3 feet high. It sometimes feeds on its mother's milk for five years, by which time it may weigh more than 1 ton.

ASIAN ELEPHANT

The Asian elephant has smaller ears and a more humped back than the African.

HOW CAN YOU TELL AN AFRICAN ELEPHANT FROM AN ASIAN ELEPHANT?

The African elephant is bigger and has larger ears and longer tusks. The head and body of the African elephant measure up to 25 feet long. The Asian elephant measures around 21 feet and has a more humped back. There is another difference at the end of the trunk. The African elephant's trunk has two flexible fingerlike lips, while the Asian animal's trunk has only one.

Large animals

After the elephant, the largest land animals are the rhinoceros, hippopotamus, and giraffe. All three live in Africa, while the rhino also lives in Asia. These mammals are plant eaters known as ungulates, which are distinguished by their hoofed feet.

HOW MANY BONES ARE THERE IN A GIRAFFE'S NECK?

A giraffe has seven bones in its neck, just like other mammals, including humans. But the giraffe's neck bones are much longer than those of other animals, and have more flexible joints in between them.

HOW TALL IS A GIRAFFE?

A male giraffe stands up to 18 feet tall to the tips of its horns. It has a very long neck, and front legs that are longer than its back legs so that the body slopes down toward the tail. The long neck allows it to feed on leaves that other animals cannot reach.

GIRAFFES

A giraffe's height allows it to watch out constantly for predators. It needs to sleep for only two hours a day.

CAN HIPPOS SWIM?

The hippo spends most of its day in or near water and comes out onto land at night to feed on plants. It is a powerful swimmer and walks on the bottom of the river at surprisingly fast speeds.

HIPPO

Hippos wallow to stay cool in the hot African sun.

WHAT IS AN OKAPI?

An okapi is a relative of the giraffe that lives in the African rain forest. It was unknown until 1900. The male has small horns on its head and a long tongue like a giraffe's, but it does not have a long neck.

IS THE RHINO ENDANGERED?

All five species of rhinoceros are endangered. The Javan rhino is the most vulnerable—only 60 animals remain. Rhinoceroses have been overhunted for their horns, which are valuable in traditional medicine.

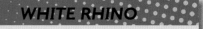

WHITE RHINO

The white rhino is actually grayish. It is also known as the square-lipped rhino.

ARE RHINOCEROSES FIERCE?

Despite their ferocious appearance and huge horns, white rhinos are usually peaceful, plant-eating animals. However, black rhinos can be ill-tempered and aggressive. If threatened, one will charge its enemy at high speed. Mothers defending their young can be particularly dangerous.

Marsupials have much shorter pregnancies than other mammals. After birth, the tiny newborns often live in a pouch on their mother's belly. Many of the 330 species of marsupial live in Australia and New Guinea.

> DO ALL MARSUPIALS HAVE A POUCH?

Most female marsupials have a pouch, but not all. Some very small marsupials such as the shrew opossums of South America do not have a pouch. Others, such as the American opossums, simply have flaps of skin around the nipples that the tiny young cling on to.

> IS A KOALA REALLY A BEAR?

No, it's a marsupial and not related to bears at all. Koalas live in Australia in eucalyptus forests. They feed almost entirely on eucalyptus leaves, preferring those of only a few species. A baby koala spends its first six or seven months in the pouch and then rides on its mother's back until it is able to fend for itself. A baby measures around ¾ of an inch at birth.

KOALA

The koala has strong claws to help it hold onto branches as it climbs in search of food.

➤ HOW MUCH DOES A KOALA EAT?

A koala eats about 18 ounces of eucalyptus leaves every day, which it chews down to a fine pulp with its broad teeth.

PLATYPUS

This unusual mammal hunts in rivers and lakes using its sensitive bill. It feeds on insects, frogs, and shrimp.

➤ WHAT IS THE SMALLEST MARSUPIAL?

The smallest marsupials are the mouselike ningauis, which live in Australia. They are only about 2 inches long.

WOMBAT

Wombats eat grasses, roots, bark, and herbs.

➤ IS A PLATYPUS A MARSUPIAL?

No, the platypus is not a marsupial, but it is an unusual animal that lives in Australia. Unlike most mammals, which give birth to live young, the platypus lays eggs. When they hatch, the young suck milk from the mother from special patches of fur.

➤ WHAT IS A WOMBAT?

A wombat is a small bearlike marsupial with a heavy body and short, strong legs. It digs burrows to shelter in, using its strong teeth and claws. Its pouch opens to the rear so that it does not fill up with earth when the wombat is burrowing.

More marsupials

More than 200 species of marsupial live in Australia and surrounding islands. There are also over 100 marsupial species in the Americas. Most of these live in South and Central America, with just the Virginia opossum native to North America.

> DO ANY MARSUPIALS SWIM?

The water opossum of South America is an excellent swimmer and has webbed back feet. Strong muscles keep its pouch closed when the opossum is in water.

> WHAT ARE BANDICOOTS?

Bandicoots are a group of small marsupials that live in Australia and New Guinea. Most have short legs, a round body, and a long, pointed nose. They have strong claws, which they use to dig for insects and other small creatures in the ground.

BANDICOOT
The bilbie bandicoot has extremely large ears to hear its insect prey.

> HOW FAST DO KANGAROOS MOVE?

A kangaroo bounds along on its strong back legs at up to 30 miles an hour. It can cover almost 45 feet in one giant bound.

TOP ? QUESTION

WHAT IS A TASMANIAN DEVIL?

The Tasmanian devil (right) is the largest of the carnivore, or flesh-eating, marsupials. It is about 35 inches long, including its tail, and has sharp teeth and strong jaws. The devil feeds mostly on carrion—the flesh of animals that are already dead—but it does also kill prey, such as birds.

> WHY DOES A KANGAROO HAVE A POUCH?

At birth, kangaroos are very tiny and poorly developed. A kangaroo is only about ¾ inch long when it is born. The female kangaroo has a pouch so that its young can complete their development in safety. The tiny newborn, called a joey, crawls up to the pouch by itself and starts to suckle on one of the nipples inside the pouch.

> WHAT DO KANGAROOS EAT?

Kangaroos eat grass and the leaves of low-growing plants, just like deer and antelopes do in the northern hemisphere.

RED KANGAROO

The largest kangaroo of all, an adult red kangaroo weighs 200 pounds.

JOEY

Joeys stay in the pouch until they weigh 20 pounds.

Monkeys >

Monkeys are members of the primate group, which also contains tarsiers, lemurs, aye-ayes, lorids, galagos, apes, and humans. Primates have large brains, hands that can form a good grip, and a tendency to walk on two legs.

HOW MANY KINDS OF MONKEY ARE THERE?

About 260 species in two main groups. One group lives in Africa and Asia. The other group lives in Central and South America.

WHICH MONKEY MAKES THE LOUDEST NOISE?

Howler monkeys shout louder than other monkeys and are among the noisiest of all animals. Their voices carry for more than 2 miles.

HOWLER MONKEY

The howler monkey spends most of its time in trees, feeding on leaves and fruit.

❯ CAN MONKEYS LIVE IN COLD PLACES?

Most monkeys are found in warm areas near to the equator, but some macaque monkeys live in cooler places. The rhesus macaque lives in the Himalayas, as well as in parts of China and India, and the Japanese macaque survives freezing winters with the help of its thick coat.

❯ WHICH IS THE BIGGEST MONKEY?

The mandrill is the largest monkey because it can grow to be 3 feet long. It lives in the tropical rain forests of Central Africa, where it hunts for insects, plants, and small animals. The smallest monkey is the pygmy marmoset of the South American rain forests. It is about 5 inches long, plus tail, and it weighs only between 3 and 5 ounces.

MACAQUES

Japanese macaques often bathe in hot springs.

GRIPPING TAIL

A prehensile tail is almost as useful as having a fifth limb.

TOP ? QUESTION

WHY DOES A MONKEY HAVE A LONG TAIL?

To help it balance and control its movements as it leaps from branch to branch in the rain forest. The tails of some South American monkeys are prehensile—they have special muscles that the monkey can use to twine around branches.

Apes >

Apes are probably the most intelligent animals in the primate group. There are three families of apes. One includes all the gibbons. The second contains the gorilla, chimpanzee, and orang-utan. And the third has only one species—humans.

> WHAT DO GORILLAS EAT?

Gorillas eat plant food, such as leaves, buds, stems, and fruit. Because their diet is juicy, gorillas rarely need to drink.

FEMALE GORILLA

Closely related to humans, gorillas are very intelligent.

> WHICH IS THE BIGGEST APE?

The gorilla. A full-grown male stands over 5½ feet tall and weighs as much as 480 pounds. Gorillas live in the forests of West and Central Africa. A family group contains one or two adult males, several females, and a number of young of different ages. The male, known as a silverback because of the white hair on his back, leads the group.

▶ DO CHIMPANZEES USE TOOLS?

Yes. The chimpanzee can get food by poking a stick into an ants' nest. It pulls out the stick and licks ` off the ants. It also uses rocks to crack nuts, and it makes sponges from chewed leaves to mop up water or wipe its body.

▶ DO CHIMPS HUNT PREY?

Yes, they do. Although fruit is the main food of chimps, they also eat insects and hunt young animals, including monkeys. They hunt alone or in a group. Groups work together, some driving a couple of animals out of the group and toward other chimps, who make the kill.

CHIMPANZEE

Chimpanzees show love toward each other and even mourn when a relative dies.

▶ WHERE DO CHIMPANZEES LIVE?

Chimpanzees live in forests and grasslands in equatorial Africa. There is another less familiar chimpanzee species called the pygmy chimpanzee, or bonobo, which lives in rain forests in Congo, Africa. It has longer limbs than the common chimpanzee and spends more of its time in trees.

WHERE DO ORANG-UTANS LIVE?

Orang-utans live in Southeast Asia, in the rain forests of Sumatra and Borneo. This ape has long, reddish fur and spends most of its life in the trees. Fruit is its main food, but the orang-utan also eats leaves, insects, and even eggs and small animals. The orang-utan is active during the day. At night it sleeps on the ground or in a nest of branches in the trees.

Lizards >

Lizards are reptiles, which means that they need to breathe air and they have skin that is covered in scales. Most lizards have four limbs and a tail. Many lizards can shed their tail to escape a predator.

KOMODO DRAGON
No predators in its habitat are large enough to take on the fierce adult Komodo dragon.

> WHICH IS THE LARGEST LIZARD?
The Komodo dragon, which lives on some Southeast Asian islands. It grows up to 10 feet long and hunts animals, such as wild pigs and small deer.

> HOW MANY KINDS OF LIZARD ARE THERE?
There are probably over 3,000 species of lizard. These belong to different groups, such as the geckos, iguanas, skinks, and chameleons. Lizards mostly live in warm parts of the world.

> ARE THERE ANY POISONOUS LIZARDS?
There are only two poisonous lizards in the world, the Gila monster (right) and the Mexican beaded lizard. Both of these live in southwestern North America. The poison is made in glands in the lower jaw. When the lizard seizes its prey and starts to chew, poison flows into the wound, and the victim soon stops struggling.

❯ WHERE DO CHAMELEONS LIVE?

There are about 85 different kinds of chameleon and most of these live in Africa and Madagascar. There are also a few Asian species and one kind of chameleon lives in parts of southern Europe.

❯ WHY DOES A CHAMELEON CHANGE COLOR?

Changing color helps the chameleon get near to its prey without being seen and allows it to hide from its enemies. The color change is controlled by the chameleon's nervous system. Nerves cause areas of color in the skin to be spread out or to become concentrated in tiny dots. Chameleons go darker when they are cold and lighter when they are hot.

❯ WHICH LIZARD SWIMS THROUGH SAND?

The sand skink lives in the sandhills of the southeastern United States. It spends most of its time below the surface, pulling itself through the sand like a swimmer moves through water.

GIVING SIGNALS

Chameleons change color not just as camouflage but as a means of communication.

CHAMELEON

The veiled chameleon can turn bright blue when it is on vivid flowers.

Like other reptiles, snakes are covered in scales. All snakes are carnivorous, which means that they feed on other animals. There are about 2,500 species of snake. They live on every continent except Antarctica, but there are no snakes in Ireland, Iceland, or New Zealand.

> HOW FAST DO SNAKES MOVE?

The fastest-moving snake on land is thought to be the black mamba, which lives in Africa. It can wriggle along at up to 7 miles an hour.

> WHICH IS THE BIGGEST SNAKE?

The world's longest snake is the reticulated python, which lives in parts of Southeast Asia. It grows to an amazing 33 feet long. The anaconda, which lives in South American rain forests, is heavier than the python but not quite as long. Pythons and anacondas are not poisonous snakes. They kill by crushing their prey to death. A python wraps the victim in the powerful coils of its body until it is suffocated.

RATTLESNAKE

If the rattle breaks, a new ring will be added when the snake molts.

> WHICH IS THE MOST DANGEROUS SNAKE?

The saw-scaled carpet viper is probably the world's most dangerous snake. It is extremely aggressive and its poison can kill humans. Saw-scaled carpet vipers live in Africa and Asia.

TOP QUESTION ?

WHY DO SNAKES SHED THEIR SKIN?

Snakes molt, or shed their skin, to make room for growth and because their skin gets worn and damaged. Some snakes, even as adults, shed their skin every 20 days.

> ARE ALL SNAKES POISONOUS?

Only about one-third of all snakes are poisonous, and fewer still have poison strong enough to harm humans. Nonpoisonous snakes either crush their prey to death or simply swallow it whole.

CAPE COBRA

The deadly Cape cobra of southern Africa can kill humans with its bite.

SNAKESKIN

Snakes wriggle out of their skin by rubbing against rough surfaces.

> WHY DOES A RATTLESNAKE RATTLE?

Rattlesnakes make their rattling noise to warn their enemies to stay far away. The rattle is made by a number of hard rings of skin at the end of the tail that make a noise when shaken. Each ring was once the tip of the tail. A new one is added every time the snake grows and sheds its skin.

Life in the water and air

Marine mammals

Not all mammals live on land. Seals, sea lions, and walruses are just some of the mammals that depend on the oceans for food. Marine mammals need to breathe air, so they have to come to the water's surface regularly. They have a thick layer of blubber, or fat, which keeps them warm in the water.

HOW FAST CAN SEALS AND SEA LIONS SWIM?

Sea lions can reach swimming speeds of 25 miles an hour. On land, the crabeater seal can reach 15 miles an hour.

HOW CAN YOU TELL A SEAL FROM A SEA LION?

With practice! Seals and sea lions both have streamlined bodies and flippers instead of limbs. But sea lions have small ear flaps, whereas seals have only ear openings. Sea lions can bring their back flippers under the body to help them move on land. Seals cannot do this—they drag themselves along.

WHICH IS THE BIGGEST SEAL?

The male elephant seal is the biggest. It is 21 feet long and weighs up to 8,000 pounds, which is as much as a small elephant.

BASKING SEAL

Seals spend a lot of their time resting on beaches between hunting trips.

❯ HOW DO SEALS KEEP WARM IN COLD SEAS?

A layer of fatty blubber under the skin helps to keep seals, sea lions, and walruses warm. The blubber may be up to 4 inches thick. These animals also have a covering of fur.

SEA LION PUP

Sea lions have external ear flaps and long front flippers.

❯ ARE BABY SEALS AND SEA LIONS BORN IN WATER?

No, they are born on land. Seals and sea lions spend most of their lives in water, but do come out onto land to give birth. They remain on land for a number of weeks, feeding their young on their rich milk.

TOP QUESTION ?

HOW BIG IS A WALRUS?

The largest male walruses (left) are more than 10 feet long and weigh 3,700 pounds. Females are smaller, averaging around 9 feet long and weighing about 1,800 pounds. The walrus's skin is about 1½ inches thick and helps protect the walrus from the tusks of others.

Whales >

Whales, dolphins, and porpoises belong to the group of marine mammals known as cetaceans. They are highly intelligent and have large tails perfect for swimming. Cetaceans breathe air through the blowhole on the top of their head.

> WHICH IS THE BIGGEST WHALE?

The blue whale is the largest whale, and also the largest mammal that has ever lived. It measures almost 100 feet long. Although it is huge, the blue whale is not a fierce hunter. It eats tiny shrimplike creatures called krill. It may gobble up as many as four million of these in a day.

> WHICH WHALE DIVES THE DEEPEST?

The sperm whale is routinely found at over 3,200 feet beneath the surface of the sea.

> HOW BIG IS A BABY BLUE WHALE?

A baby blue whale is about 26 feet long at birth and is the biggest baby in the animal kingdom.

BALEEN PLATES

A right whale skims the sea for krill, showing its baleen plates.

❯ HOW DOES A BLUE WHALE FEED?

Hanging from the whale's upper jaw are a lot of plates of a bristly material called baleen. The whale opens its mouth and water full of krill flows in. The water flows out at the sides of the mouth, leaving the krill behind on the baleen for the whale to swallow.

❯ WHY DO SOME WHALES MIGRATE?

Whales, such as humpbacks, migrate—travel seasonally— to find the best conditions for feeding and breeding. They spend much of the year feeding in the waters of the Arctic and Antarctic, where there is plenty of krill to eat. When it is time to give birth, the humpbacks travel to warmer waters near the equator.

❯ DO HUMPBACK WHALES SING?

Yes, they do. They make a series of sounds, including high whistles and low rumbles, that may last from 5 to 35 minutes. No one knows why the humpback whale sings, but it may be to court a mate or to keep in touch with others in the group.

HUMPBACK WHALE

Whales often "breach," flinging themselves out of the water and landing with a noisy splash.

More whales >

There are two groups of whales: toothed whales and whales that catch food with baleen filters. Dolphins and porpoises are toothed, while blue and humpback whales are baleen whales.

> ## DO WHALES EVER COME TO LAND?

No, whales spend their whole lives in the sea. But they do breathe air and surface regularly to take breaths.

> ## IS A DOLPHIN A WHALE?

A dolphin is a small whale. Most of the 32 or so species of dolphin live in the sea, but there are 5 species that live in rivers. The biggest dolphin is the killer whale (left), which grows up to 32 feet long. Dolphins have a streamlined shape and a beaked snout containing sharp teeth.

SPY HOPPING

Dolphins often "spy hop," coming to the surface to look around.

❯ DO WHALES GIVE BIRTH IN WATER?

Yes, they do. The baby whale comes out of the mother's body tail first so that it does not drown during birth. As soon as the head emerges, the mother and the other females attending the birth help the baby swim to the surface to take its first breath.

❯ WHAT IS A PORPOISE?

A porpoise is a small whale with a rounded head, not a beaked snout like a dolphin. There are six species of porpoise. They live in coastal waters in the Atlantic, Pacific, and Indian oceans. Like other toothed whales, the porpoise uses echolocation to find its prey. It gives off a series of high-pitched clicking sounds and the echoes tell the porpoise its prey's direction.

❯ HOW FAST DO WHALES SWIM?

Blue whales can move at speeds of up to 20 miles an hour when disturbed. Some small whales, such as pilot whales and dolphins, may swim at more than 30 miles an hour.

COMMON DOLPHIN

Dolphins are fast swimmers and catch squid and fish to eat.

WHAT IS A NARWHAL?

∨

A narwhal is a whale with a single long tusk at the front of its head. The tusk is actually a tooth, which grows out from the upper jaw. It can be as much as 10 feet long. Only male narwhals have tusks. They may use them in battles with other males.

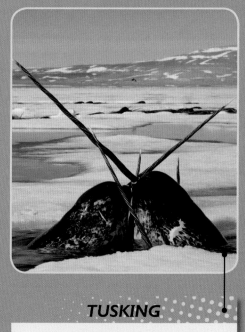

TUSKING

These narwhals are "tusking," or rubbing their tusks together.

Sharks and rays >

Sharks and rays belong to a group of fish that have skeletons made of cartilage instead of bone. Cartilage is softer and more flexible than bone. Sharks and rays also have much larger brains than other types of fish. Sharks are the ocean's most feared predators.

HOW MANY KINDS OF SHARK ARE THERE?

There are over 300 different species of shark living all over the world. They range in size from dwarf dogfish measuring only 8 inches long to the giant whale shark, which can grow to 50 feet.

ARE ALL SHARKS KILLERS?

No, two of the largest sharks, the whale shark and the basking shark, eat only tiny shrimplike creatures. They filter these from the water through strainerlike structures in the mouth.

HOW BIG IS A GREAT WHITE SHARK?

Great white sharks (right) are mostly about 23 feet long, but some can grow up to 40 feet. They live in warm seas all over the world. Great white sharks are fierce hunters and attack large fish and creatures, such as sea lions and porpoises. Their main weapons are their large, jagged-edge teeth.

TIGER SHARKS

These sharks prey on fish, seals, birds, turtles, and other sharks.

> HOW FAST DO SHARKS SWIM?

A shark is able to swim at speeds of up to 25 miles an hour for short periods.

> DOES A STINGRAY STING?

A stingray gets its name from the sharp spine near the base of its tail. The stingray lives in warm, shallow waters, where its spine can cause a nasty wound if stepped on.

STINGRAY

The blue-spotted stingray is up to 27 inches wide.

Fish

Fish live in all the world's bodies of water, from mountain streams to the depths of the oceans. Fish have streamlined bodies ideal for swimming through water. Most fish are covered in scales to provide protection from predators.

> WHAT IS AN ANEMONEFISH?

Anemonefish live in sea anemones that thrive in tropical waters. Sea anemones are related to jellyfish and have a powerful sting. Anemonefish are the only fish that are immune to the poison, so they can hide from predators in their host.

> HOW FAST DO FISH SWIM?

The sailfish is one of the fastest-swimming fish. It can move at speeds of more than 70 miles an hour. Marlins and tunas are also fast swimmers. All these fish have sleek, streamlined bodies.

ANEMONEFISH

The clown anemonefish hides among anemone tentacles.

PIRANHA

Piranhas are known for their triangular-shape teeth.

TOP QUESTION ?

WHICH IS THE FIERCEST FRESH-WATER FISH?

The piranha, which lives in rivers in tropical South America, is the fiercest of all freshwater fish. Each fish is only about 10 to 24 inches long, but a shoal of hundreds attacking together can kill and eat a large mammal very quickly. The piranha's weapons are its extremely sharp, flesh-ripping teeth.

➤ ARE ELECTRIC EELS REALLY ELECTRIC?

Yes, they are. The electric eel's body contains special muscles that can release electrical charges into the water. These are powerful enough to stun its prey.

➤ WHY DOES A FLYING FISH "FLY"?

A flying fish usually lifts itself above the water to escape from danger. It has extralarge fins, which act as "wings." After building up speed under the water, the fish lifts its fins and glides above the surface for a short distance.

PUFFER FISH

This fish puffs up its body when it is threatened.

➤ ARE THERE ANY POISONOUS FISH IN THE SEA?

Yes, and the puffer fish is one of the most poisonous of all. It has a powerful poison in some of its internal organs, such as the liver, which can kill a human. Despite this, carefully prepared puffer fish is a delicacy in Japan.

Amphibians >

Unlike other land animals, most amphibians lay their eggs in water. Young amphibians live and breathe in water, before transforming into air-breathing and land-living adults.

> HOW CAN TREE FROGS CLIMB TREES?

Tree frogs are excellent climbers. On each of their long toes is a round sticky pad, which allows them to cling to the undersides of leaves and to run up the smoothest surfaces. Tree frogs spend most of their lives in trees, catching insects to eat, and may only come down to the ground to lay their eggs in or near water.

> WHY DO FROGS CROAK?

Male frogs make their croaking calls to attract females. The frog has a special sac of skin under its chin, which blows up and helps make the call louder.

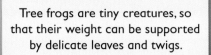

TREE FROG

Tree frogs are tiny creatures, so that their weight can be supported by delicate leaves and twigs.

TOE PAD

This frog has enlarged toe pads and long fingers and toes perfect for climbing.

TADPOLE

As tadpoles mature, they slowly grow limbs.

❯ WHAT IS A TADPOLE?

A tadpole is the larva, or young, of an amphibian, such as a frog or newt. The amphibian egg is usually laid in water and hatches out into a small, swimming creature with a long tail called a tadpole. The tadpole feeds on water plants and gradually develops into its adult form.

❯ WHICH IS THE SMALLEST FROG?

The smallest frog, and the smallest of all amphibians, is the Cuban frog, which measures less than ½ inch long. The tiny gold frog, which lives in Brazilian rain forests, is probably about the same size.

❯ HOW MANY TYPES OF FROG AND TOAD ARE THERE?

There may be as many as 4,000 species of frog and toad. They live on all continents except Antarctica. Most live in areas with plenty of rainfall, but some manage to live in drier lands by sheltering in burrows.

FROGS' EGGS

Many frog species release thousands of eggs at a time.

❯ DO ALL FROGS LAY THEIR EGGS IN WATER?

No, some frogs have very unusual breeding habits. The male marsupial frog (and sometimes the female) carries his mate's eggs in a pouch on his back or hip. The male Darwin's frog keeps his mate's eggs in his vocal pouch until they have developed into tiny frogs.

Crocodiles and alligators >

Crocodiles and alligators are water-dwelling reptiles that live in tropical climates. They have sharp teeth and very powerful jaws. These reptiles also have streamlined bodies and strong legs, so they can move very fast, in and out of water.

> WHAT DO CROCODILES EAT?

Baby crocodiles start by catching insects and spiders to eat. As they grow, fish and birds form a larger part of their diet. Full-grown crocodiles prey on anything that comes their way, even large animals, such as giraffes.

> WHICH IS THE BIGGEST CROCODILE?

The Nile crocodile grows up to 20 feet long, but the Indopacific crocodile, which lives in parts of Southeast Asia, may be even larger.

> HOW MANY TYPES OF CROCODILE ARE THERE?

There are 14 species of crocodile, 2 species of alligator, several species of caiman, and 1 species of gavial. The gavial is very similar to the crocodile and the alligator, with a long, slender snout.

NILE CROCODILE

The crocodile is armored with rows of scales.

TOP QUESTION ?

DO CROCODILES LAY EGGS?

Crocodiles do lay eggs and they take care of them very carefully. Most female crocodiles dig a pit into which they lay 30 or more eggs. They cover them over with earth or sand. While the eggs incubate for about three months, the female crocodile stays nearby guarding the nest.

➤ ARE CROCODILES AN ANCIENT SPECIES?

Crocodiles have looked the same since the time of the dinosaurs. They are 200 million years old.

➤ HOW CAN YOU TELL A CROCODILE FROM AN ALLIGATOR?

Crocodiles and alligators are very similar, but you can recognize a crocodile because its teeth stick out when its mouth is shut! In alligators, the fourth pair of teeth on the lower jaw disappears into pits in the upper jaw, but in crocodiles, these teeth slide outside the mouth.

ALLIGATOR AGGRESSION

Adult alligators get into frequent battles to defend their territory.

Aquatic reptiles >

Crocodiles are not the only reptiles that live in oceans, rivers, and lakes. Aquatic turtles spend most of their lives in water, coming to land to lay eggs. Their bodies are protected by a hard, bony shell. They cannot breathe in water, so must come to the surface for air.

HAWKSBILL TURTLE

The hawksbill turtle is one of the few creatures that feeds mostly on sea sponges.

› WHICH IS THE BIGGEST TURTLE?

The leatherback is the largest of all the turtles. It grows up to 5½ feet long and weighs up to 800 pounds. Leatherback turtles can usually be seen far out at sea.

▶ ARE THERE SNAKES IN THE SEA?

Yes, there are 50 to 60 species of snake that spend their whole lives in the sea. They eat fish and other sea creatures and all are extremely poisonous. One species, the beaked sea snake, is potentially lethal.

› WHAT DO SEA TURTLES EAT?

Most sea turtles eat a range of underwater creatures, such as clams, shrimp, and snails, but some concentrate on certain foods. For example, the green turtle eats mainly sea grass.

WHERE DO SEA TURTLES LAY THEIR EGGS?

Female sea turtles dig a pit on a sandy beach in which to lay their eggs. They then cover the eggs with sand. When the young hatch, they dig their way out and struggle to the sea.

GIANT FLIPPERS

The female hawksbill uses its flippers for swimming and for digging nests.

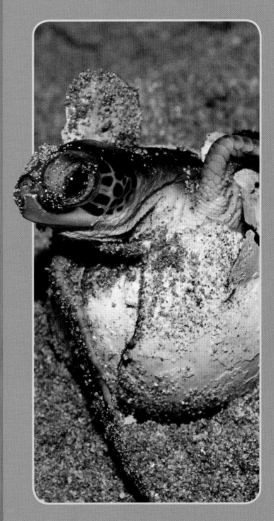

› DO TURTLES LIVE IN FRESHWATER?

Yes, there are about 200 species of freshwater turtles living throughout the world's warmer regions.

Polar birds >

Few animals are able to survive in the harsh climates of the Arctic and Antarctic. Some hardy birds travel to the polar regions to breed during the relatively warm summers. Some penguin species are able to withstand the bitter Antarctic cold.

> WHICH IS THE BIGGEST PENGUIN?

The emperor penguin lives in Antarctica and is the biggest penguin in the world. It stands about 45 inches tall. Like all penguins, it cannot fly, but it is an expert swimmer and diver, using its wings as paddles. It spends most of its life in the water, where it catches fish and squid to eat.

> DO ALL PENGUINS LIVE IN ANTARCTICA?

Most of the 18 species of penguin live in or near Antarctica, but some are found in warmer areas, such as around New Zealand. There are no penguins in the northern hemisphere.

> HOW FAST DO PENGUINS SWIM?

Penguins can swim at speeds of 8 miles an hour, but they may move even faster for short periods. Some penguins are able to stay under water for up to 20 minutes.

EMPEROR PENGUIN COLONY

Emperor penguins come to land to breed. The female lays an egg that the male keeps warm on his feet for about 60 days until it hatches.

➤ WHICH BIRD MAKES THE LONGEST MIGRATION?

The Arctic tern makes the longest migration journey of any bird. Each year it makes a round trip of 22,000 miles. The birds nest in the Arctic during the northern summer and then travel south to escape the northern winter, spending the southern summer near Antarctica, where food is plentiful.

ARCTIC TERN

These long-lived birds can survive for up to 20 years.

➤ WHICH BIRD HAS THE LONGEST WINGS?

The wandering albatross has the longest wings of any bird. When fully spread, they measure up to 11 feet. This majestic seabird lays its eggs and cares for its young on islands near Antarctica.

TOP QUESTION ?

WHICH IS THE SMALLEST PENGUIN?

The little, or fairy, penguin is the smallest penguin. It is only about 15 inches long. It lives in waters off the coasts of New Zealand and Tasmania, Australia.

Birds >

There are around 10,000 different species of bird. They inhabit every one of the world's ecosystems, from deserts to rain forests. Birds have feathers, a beak, and wings. All birds lay hard-shell eggs.

> HOW MANY KINDS OF GULL ARE THERE?

There are about 45 species of gull. They live in all parts of the world, but there are more species north of the equator. Gulls range in size from the little gull, which is only 11 inches long, to the great black-backed gull, a huge 25 inches long. Many gulls find food inland as well as at sea.

GANNET
Gannets are the largest seabirds in the North Atlantic Ocean, with a wingspan of up to 6½ feet.

> HOW DOES A GANNET CATCH ITS FOOD?

The gannet catches fish and squid in spectacular dives into the sea. This seabird flies over the water looking for prey. When it sees something, it plunges from as high as 100 feet above the ocean, dives into the water with its wings swept back, and seizes the catch in its daggerlike beak.

PUFFIN
Puffins have black-and-white plumage and display a colorful beak when breeding.

> IS A PUFFIN A KIND OF PENGUIN?

No, puffins belong to a different family of birds, called auks. They live in the northern hemisphere, particularly around the Arctic. Auks are good swimmers and divers, like penguins, but can also fly, which penguins cannot do.

> HOW MANY SPECIES OF PARROT ARE THERE?

There are about 350 species of parrot, all of which live in the warmer regions of the world. Parrots have a strong, curved beak and many species are brightly colored. Parrots are among the most intelligent birds and can be trained to mimic human speech.

> WHY DOES A PELICAN HAVE A POUCH?

The pelican has a pouch to help it catch fish to eat. When the bird plunges its open beak into the water, the pouch fills up with water and fish. As it brings its head up again, the water drains from the pouch, leaving any fish behind to be swallowed.

MACAWS

The scarlet macaw is a parrot that lives in the forests of Central and South America.

> WHAT IS A TROPIC BIRD?

A tropic bird is a seabird with two very long, central tail feathers. There are three species, all of which fly over tropical oceans.

Birds of prey >

Birds of prey are hunters, feeding on small animals from insects to fish and mammals. They often make use of keen eyesight and sharp hearing, while their strong beaks and claws are ideal for tearing into flesh.

> DO EAGLES CATCH SNAKES?

Yes, snake eagles feed on snakes and lizards. The rough surface of the eagle's toes helps it hold onto slippery snakes.

GRIFFON VULTURE

The vulture's bald head is ideal for feeding in messy carcasses.

> DO VULTURES HUNT AND KILL PREY?

Vultures do not usually kill their prey. They are scavengers, feeding on animals that are already dead or have been killed by hunters, such as lions. They have strong claws and beaks, and their bald head allows them to plunge into carcasses without matting their feathers.

> WHICH VULTURE IS A BONE CRACKER?

The bearded vulture picks up bones and drops them from a great height onto rocks. This smashes them open, so the bird can feed on the marrow inside.

PEREGRINE FALCON

This falcon likes to feed on birds, plus small mammals and reptiles.

> WHICH IS THE FASTEST BIRD?

As it dives to catch other birds in the air, the peregrine falcon may move at about 200 miles an hour, faster than any other bird. The falcon circles above its victim before making its fast dive and killing the prey on impact.

> HOW CAN OWLS HUNT AT NIGHT?

Owls have excellent sight, even in low light, and very sharp hearing. Owls also have special soft-edged wing feathers that make very little noise as they beat their wings, swooping down on their unsuspecting prey.

HOW MANY KINDS OF OWL ARE THERE?

There are 145 species of owl in two families. The barn owl family contains about 10 species and the true owl family about 135 species. Owls live in most parts of the world, except a few islands. They usually hunt at night, catching small mammals, birds, frogs, lizards, insects, and even fish.

More birds of prey >

There are about 500 species of birds of prey, including eagles, hawks, buzzards, harriers, kites, falcons, and vultures. All these birds hunt during the day and rest at night. The only nocturnal birds of prey are the owls.

OSPREYS

Ospreys share a small fish in their nest, which is made of a heap of sticks and seaweed.

> WHICH IS THE SMALLEST BIRD OF PREY?

The black-legged falconet and the Bornean falconet, of Southeast Asia, both have an average length of 5½–6 inches. They feed on small birds and insects.

> WHAT DOES AN OSPREY EAT?

The osprey feeds mostly on fish. When it sees something near the surface, it dives down toward the water and seizes the fish in its feet. The soles of its feet are covered with small spines to help it hold onto the slippery fish.

> WHICH IS THE BIGGEST EAGLE?

The biggest eagle in the world is the great harpy eagle, from the rain forests of South America. It is up to 3 feet long. It hunts monkeys and sloths in the trees, chasing them from branch to branch.

➤ WHICH IS THE BIGGEST BIRD OF PREY?

The Andean condor is the biggest bird of prey in the world. It measures up to 43 inches long and weighs up to 26 pounds. Its huge wingspan is over 10 feet across.

DO EAGLES BUILD NESTS?

Yes, and the nest, called an eyrie (above), made by the bald eagle is the biggest made by any bird, at up to 18 feet deep. They are used again and again, with the eagles adding more nesting material each year.

ANDEAN CONDOR

The Andean condor's face is nearly featherless, but it has a ruff of white feathers around its neck.

➤ HOW DO EAGLES KILL THEIR PREY?

An eagle kills with the four long, curved claws on each of its feet. It drops down onto its prey, seizes it in its long talons, and crushes it to death. The eagle then tears the flesh apart with its strong hooked beak.

Glossary

Aboriginal
One of the original inhabitants of Australia. Aboriginals were already there when European settlers arrived.

Aquatic
Something that lives in water.

Atmosphere
A layer of gas held around a planet by gravity. The earth's atmosphere is over 500 miles thick.

Beak
The jaws of a bird, made of bone, which it uses for feeding.

Camouflage
Coloring that allows an animal to blend in with its background.

Carnivore
An animal that eats other animals.

Cell
The tiny unit from which all bodies are made. The smallest animals have just one cell, and the largest have many millions.

Climate
The pattern of weather in an area. All plants and animals are suited to their native climate.

Colony
A group of animals living together in a shared home.

Continent
One of the earth's seven large land areas, which are Africa, Antarctica, Asia, Australia, Europe, North America, and South America.

Crustacean
An animal without a backbone that has a body covered by an outer skeleton. Crustaceans include crabs, lobsters, crayfish, shrimp, krill, and barnacles.

Democracy
A system of government in which leaders are chosen by people in elections. A government in which the leader is not elected is called a dictatorship.

Desert
An area of land that receives little rain. As life needs water to survive, fewer plants and animals live in deserts.

Endangered
A species, or kind, of animal that is so few in number that it is in danger of disappearing.

Equator
An imaginary line that runs round the middle of the earth.

Evolution
The process by which animals and plants adapt and change over many generations. Those that are best suited to their surroundings survive and produce young, while others die out.

Extinction
When a species can no longer survive due to overhunting or when there is a change in its habitat.

Fin
A part of the body of a fish that is used for swimming.

Fossil
The remains of an animal or plant that has been preserved in rock or another substance, often for millions of years.

Greenhouse effect
The warming of the earth, also known as "global warming," due to the presence of the gas carbon dioxide in the air, which stops heat escaping from the atmosphere. Pollution from burning oil and coal is causing an increase in the greenhouse effect.

Habitat
The place where an animal or plant lives.

Herbivore
An animal that eats only plants.

Herd
A large group of hoofed mammals that live together.

Hibernation
A sleep that some animals go into to survive the winter. The animal's heart rate slows down.

Ice caps
The layers of ice and snow that cover the North and South poles.

Incubation
Keeping eggs warm so that they will hatch successfully.

Insect
An animal without a backbone that has three body parts, three pairs of legs, and usually two pairs of wings.

Magma
The molten, or liquid, rock under the surface of the earth that sometimes rises up through volcanoes.

Mammal
An animal with a backbone that usually has hair on its skin. Female mammals make milk to feed their young.

Microscopic
Too small to be seen with the naked eye.

Middle Ages
A period in history that is often defined as spanning from around AD 500 to 1500.

Migration
A regular journey made by an animal.

Nocturnal
When an animal is active at night and rests during the day.

Omnivore
An animal that eats both plants and animals.

Photosynthesis
The process plants use to make chemicals using the sun's energy. This forms the basis for all other life as it is the only way in nature to take energy from the sun.

Polar
Related to the cold areas around the North and South poles.

Population
The total number of people or animals living in a particular place.

Predator
An animal that hunts and eats other animals.

Prey
An animal that is hunted by another animal for food.

Rain forest
Dense forest found in areas with high rainfall around the equator.

Renewable energy
A source of energy, such as wind power, which cannot be used up.

Reptile
An animal with a backbone that has four legs and a body covered by scales.

Satellite
Any object that orbits a planet, held by the planet's gravity.

Scavenger
An animal that eats dead plants or animals.

Sediment
Small pieces of rock or soil that settle at the bottom of rivers and oceans.

Senses
The ways humans and animals are able to experience the world around them. Humans have five senses: sight, hearing, touch, smell, and taste.

Shoal
A group of fish that swim together.

Skeleton
The framework of a body that holds it together. Some skeletons are inside the body, while others are outside.

Streamlined
When something is smooth and tapered and can move through water or air with very little effort.

Temperate
Areas of the world that have a mild climate and four seasons.

Tentacle
A long, feelerlike structure found on certain animals, such as jellyfish.

Tradition
A way of doing things, such as making music, cooking, or a system of government, that is passed down from one generation to another.

Tropical
Areas of the world that lie around the middle of the earth, near the equator, and are hot all year round.

Tusk
An extra-long tooth found on some animals, such as elephants.

Venom
A harmful liquid that some animals make to kill prey or to defend themselves.

Vertebrate
Any animal that has a bony skeleton and a backbone. Animals without a backbone are called invertebrate.

Index

A-knowledgments →

t = top, b = bottom, l = left, r = right, m = middle

1 Denise Kappa/iStockphoto, 2 Christophe Testi/Dreamstime.com, 3 Scheiker/Dreamstime.com, 4–5 Eric Meola/The Image Bank/Getty Images, 6–7 Nick Schlax/iStockphoto, 8–9 Robert Everts/Getty Images, 10–11 Alessandro Bolis/Dreamstime.com, 11l Webking/Dreamstime.com, 11r Karen Moller/iStockphoto, 12–13 Jeremy Walker/Getty Images, 12 Moemrik/Dreamstime.com, 13 James Steidl/Dreamstime.com, 14–15 Philippe Bourseiller/Getty Images, 15t Denise Kappa/iStockphoto, 15b European/Getty Images, 16–17 Pavalache Stelian/Dreamstime.com, 17t Robyvannucci/Dreamstime.com, 17b Carolyne Pehora/Dreamstime.com, 18 David Pedre/iStockphoto, 19t Norbert Speicher/iStockphoto, 19b French School/Getty Images, 20–21 Robert Churchill/iStockphoto, 21l David Lentz/iStockphoto, 21r Jason Gulledge/iStockphoto, 22 DaddyBit/iStockphoto, 23t George Gower/Getty Images, 23b Erick Nguyen/Dreamstime.com, 24–25 Mike Carlson/Dreamstime.com, 25t Luciano Mortula/Dreamstime.com, 25b Rb-studio/Dreamstime.com, 26 Mansell/Time & Life Pictures/Getty Images, 27l William Wang/Dreamstime.com, 27r Matthew Scholey/Dreamstime.com, 28 Sundown/Dreamstime.com, 29t Michael Thompson/Dreamstime.com, 29b Coomerguy/Dreamstime.com, 30–31 Time Life Pictures/Mansell/Getty Images, 30 English School/Getty Images, 31 Rod Lawson/Dreamstime.com, 32t Dan Braus Photography/iStockphoto, 32b Popperfoto/Getty Images, 33 NASA, 34–35 Greg Wood/AFP/Getty Images, 36–37 Joshua Haviv/iStockphoto, 36 Eric Feferberg/AFP/Getty Images, 37 Robert Churchill/iStockphoto, 38l Steffen Foerster/Dreamstime.com, 38r Jerry Cooke/Pix Inc./Time Life Pictures/Getty Images, 39 DNDavis/Dreamstime.com, 40–41 Bruce Hempell/Dreamstime.com, 41 Asdf_1/Dreamstime.com, 42–43 Denis Babenko/Dreamstime.com, 43t Joel Blit/Dreamstime.com, 43b iStockphoto, 44t English School/Bridgeman/Getty Images, 44b Richard Simkin/Bridgeman/Getty Images, 45 Sygma/Corbis, 46 Franck Fife/AFP/Getty Images, 47t Graeme Robertson/Getty Images, 47b Marekuliasz/Dreamstime.com, 48 Stougard/Dreamstime.com, 49t Natalia Bratslavsky/Dreamstime.com, 49b Maria Weidner/iStockphoto, 50t Paul Moore/Dreamstime.com, 50b Brailean/Dreamstime.com, 51 Stoffies01/Dreamstime.com, 52 Christopher Howey/Dreamstime.com, 52–53 Elpis Ioannidis/Dreamstime.com, 53 Itinerantlens/Dreamstime.com, 54t Webking/Dreamstime.com, 54b Tiburonstudios/Dreamstime.com, 55 Tall Tree Ltd, 56t Karen Winton/Dreamstime.com, 56b Alena Yakusheva/Dreamstime.com, 57 Chris Harvey/Dreamstime.com, 58 Will Sanders/Getty Images, 58–59 Dreamstime.com, 59 Nivi/Dreamstime.com, 60–61 Eric Meola/The Image Bank/Getty Images, 62–63 Tiero/Dreamstime.com, 63t iStockphoto, 63b Lambert (Bart) Parren/Dreamstime.com, 64–65 Aidar Ayazbayev/iStockphoto, 64 Craig Hanson/Dreamstime.com, 65 Catherine Jones/Dreamstime.com, 66–67 Nikhil Gangavane/Dreamstime.com, 67t Howard Sandler/iStockphoto, 67b Christophe Testi/Dreamstime.com, 68l Shawn O'Banion/iStockphoto, 68r Adriana Barsanti/iStockphoto, 69 Jose Gil/Dreamstime.com, 70 Pavel Aleynikov/Dreamstime.com, 71t Bruno Vincent/Getty Images, 71b Paula Connelly/iStockphoto, 72t Paul Gauguin/The Bridgeman Art Library/Getty Images, 72b Museum of New Mexico, 73 Oliver Strewe/Lonely Planet Images/Getty Images, 74–75 Vojko Kavcic/Dreamstime.com, 75t Edward Shaw/iStockphoto, 75b Monkey Business Images/Dreamstime.com, 76 Ioana Grecu/Dreamstime.com, 77t Daria Khlopkina/Dreamstime.com, 77b Will Hayward/Dreamstime.com, 78–79 Shariff Che' Lah/Dreamstime.com, 78 Alan Tobey/iStockphoto, 79 Eric Ryan/Getty Images, 80t iStockphoto, 80b Terraxplorer/iStockphoto, 81 Pierdelune/Dreamstime.com, 82–83 Andrew Buckin/Dreamstime.com, 83l Pcphotos/Dreamstime.com, 83r Bananaman/Dreamstime.com, 84–85 Daniel Boiteau/Dreamstime.com, 85t iStockphoto, 85b Jakich/Dreamstime.com, 86–87 Richard Bouhet/AFP/Getty Images, 88 Antonio Petrone/Dreamstime.com, 89 O. Louis Mazzatenta/National Geographic/Getty Images, 90 and 90–91 Bob Aimsworth/Dreamstime.com, 91 Kevin Walsh/Dreamstime.com, 92–93 Paul Prescott/Dreamstime.com, 94–95 Panoramic Images/Getty Images, 95 Randall L. Ricklefs/McDonald Observatory, 96 Archive Holdings Inc./Getty Images, 97t Dario Mitidieri/Reportage/Getty Images, 97b iStockphoto, 98–99 Julien Grondin/iStockphoto.com, 99l Adeline Yeo Hwee Ching/Dreamstime.com, 99r Snem/Dreamstime.com, 100 Andy Butler/Dreamstime.com, 101t Scott Rothstein/Dreamstime.com, 101b J. Duggan/Dreamstime.com, 102t Piotr Majka/Dreamstime.com, 102m Fabrizio Argonauta/Dreamstime.com, 102b Evgeny Terentyev/iStockphoto, 103 Pavlos Rekas/Dreamstime.com, 104–105 Tanya Weliky/Dreamstime.com, 105t Bob Aimsworth/Dreamstime.com, 105b Ismael Montero/Dreamstime.com, 106–107 iStockphoto, 107t Mark Kostich/iStockphoto, 107b Popperfoto/Getty Images, 108–109 Kazuyoshi Nomachi/Corbis, 108 and 109 iStockphoto, 110 NASA, 110–111 William Britten/iStockphoto, 111 Alexal/Dreamstime.com, 112–113 Frank Krahmer/Getty Images, 114–115 Chenyhscut/Dreamstime.com, 114 Pancaketom/Dreamstime.com, 115 Joe Gough/iStockphoto, 116–117 Joshua Haviv/iStockphoto, 116 Pierdelune/Dreamstime.com, 117l Jack Dykinga/Getty Images, 117r Joshua Lurie-Terrell/iStockphoto, 118–119 Grafissimo/iStockphoto, 118 Petra Klaassen/Dreamstime.com, 119 NASA, 120–121 Peter Clark/Dreamstime.com, 121t Joe Gough/Dreamstime.com, 121b Stuart Elflett/Dreamstime.com, 122–123 Dr Marli Miller/Getty Images, 122 Reinhard Tiburzy/Dreamstime.com, 123 Dmitry Kozlov/Dreamstime.com, 124–125t Joe Cornish/Getty Images, 124–125b Andreas Sandberg/iStockphoto, 125 Alexander Potapov/Dreamstime.com, 126 Vladimir Kondrachov/iStockphoto, 126–127 Howardliuphoto/Dreamstime.com, 127 Hashim Pudiyapura/Dreamstime.com, 128–129 Alexander Hafemann/iStockphoto, 128 Armin Rose/Dreamstime.com, 129 Anthony Hathaway/Dreamstime.com, 130–131 Daniel Stein/iStockphoto, 130 Corbis, 131 Wolfgang Amri/Dreamstime.com, 132 Jonathan White/iStockphoto, 133t Dave Raboin/iStockphoto, 133b Wessel Cirkel/Dreamstime.com, 134–135 Nick Schlax/iStockphoto, 135t Robyn Mackenzie/Dreamstime.com, 135b Spunky1234/Dreamstime.com, 136 Oksana Asai/Dreamstime.com, 137l Francois Etienne Du Plessis/Dreamstime.com, 137r Dirk-Jan Mattaar/Dreamstime.com, 138–139 Adam Jones/Visuals Unlimited/Getty Images, 140 Peter Garbet/iStockphoto, 141t Ppmaker2007/Dreamstime.com, 141b Richard Griffin/Dreamstime.com, 142 Mikeexpert/Dreamstime.com, 143l Janehb/Dreamstime.com, 143r Tommounsey/Dreamstime.com, 144 Liang Ma/Dreamstime.com, 145t Karoline Cullen/Dreamstime.com, 145b Scheiker/Dreamstime.com, 146–147 Gumenuk Vitalij/Dreamstime.com, 147t Brenda A. Smith/Dreamstime.com, 147b Bill Kennedy/Dreamstime.com, 148 Isabel Poulin/Dreamstime.com, 149l Tessa Rath/Dreamstime.com, 149r Colleen Coombe/Dreamstime.com, 150 Larry Ye/Dreamstime.com, 151t Sandra Cunningham/Dreamstime.com, 151b Laura Bulau/Dreamstime.com, 152l Angela Vetu/Dreamstime.com, 152r Oneclearvision/iStockphoto, 153 Rene Hoffmann/Dreamstime.com, 154 Chris Hellier/Corbis, 155t Kai Zhang/Dreamstime.com, 155b Carrie Bottomley/iStockphoto, 156 Peter Elvidge/Dreamstime.com, 157t Feng Hui/Dreamstime.com, 157b Pasticcio/iStockphoto, 158–159 Marek Cech/iStockphoto, 159t Peter Pattavina/iStockphoto, 159b Mark Kolbe/iStockphoto, 160 Maxim Malevich/Dreamstime.com, 161l Ken Cole/Dreamstime.com, 161r Dean Pennala/Dreamstime.com, 162 Vova Pomortzeff/Dreamstime.com, 162–163 Lesya Castillo/Dreamstime.com, 163 Alan T. Duffy 1970/Dreamstime.com, 164–165 Ronald Wittek/Getty Images, 166–167 Ken Cole/Dreamstime.com and John Pitcher/iStockphoto, 166 Sters/Dreamstime.com, 167 Ryszard Laskowski/Dreamstime.com, 168 Anthony Hathaway/Dreamstime.com, 169l Valerie Crafter/iStockphoto, 169r Sandra vom Stein/iStockphoto, 170 Kitch Bain/iStockphoto, 171l Karel Broz/Dreamstime.com, 171r Anita Huszti/iStockphoto, 172t Yong Chen/Dreamstime.com, 172b Jean-Marc Strydom/Dreamstime.com, 173 Ian Jeffery/iStockphoto, 174–175 Neil Bradfield/iStockphoto, 174 Edward Duckitt/Dreamstime.com, 175 Jayanand Govindaraj/Dreamstime.com, 176 Chris Fourie/Dreamstime.com, 177t Romkaz/Dreamstime.com, 177b Lee Dirden/Dreamstime.com, 178 Yegor Korzh/Dreamstime.com, 179t Nicole Duplaix/National Geographic/Getty Images, 179b Gary Unwin/Dreamstime.com, 180 Martin Harvey/Corbis, 181l Ewan Chesser/Dreamstime.com, 181r Rusty Dodson/Dreamstime.com, 182 Eric Delmar/iStockphoto, 183t Can Balcioglu/Dreamstime, 183b Xavier Marchant/Dreamstime.com, 184 Eric Gevaert/Dreamstime.com, 185l Peter-John Freeman/iStockphoto, 185r George Clerk/iStockphoto, 186t Anna Yu/iStockphoto, 186b Hudakore/Dreamstime.com, 187 Sebastian Duda/iStockphoto, 188 Paul McCormick/Getty Images, 189l Joe McDaniel/iStockphoto, 189r Nico Smit/Dreamstime.com, 190–191 Tim Laman/National Geographic/Getty Images, 192 Tom Dowd/Dreamstime.com, 193t Morten Elm/iStockphoto, 193b John Pitcher/iStockphoto, 194 Jens Kuhfs/Getty Images, 195t Ken Moore/Dreamstime.com, 195b Dale Walsh/iStockphoto, 196 Evgeniya Lazareva/iStockphoto, 196–197 David Schrader/iStockphoto, 197 Paul Nicklen/National Geographic/Getty Images, 198 Romilly Lockyer/Getty Images, 198–199 Jeff Hunter/Getty Images, 199 Casey and Astrid Witte Mahaney/Lonely Planet Images/Getty Images, 200 Carol Buchanan/Dreamstime.com, 201t Jacek Chabraszewski/Dreamstime.com, 201b Sergey Kulikov/iStockphoto, 202 Mark Kostich/iStockphoto, 203t Tommounsey/Dreamstime.com, 203b iStockphoto, 204 Greg Niemi/iStockphoto, 205t Anup Shah/The Image Bank/Getty Images, 205b Mark Higgins/iStockphoto, 206 Kim Bunker/iStockphoto, 207 Jason Edwards/National Geographic/Getty Images, 208–209 Kim Bunker/iStockphoto, 209t Jerome Whittingham/Dreamstime.com, 209b Thomas Bjornstad/Dreamstime.com, 210t Janne Hämäläinen/iStockphoto, 210b Paul Edwards/Dreamstime.com, 211 Roberto A. Sanchez/iStockphoto, 212–213 iStockphoto, 213l Andrew Howe/iStockphoto, 213r Rui Saraiva/Dreamstime.com, 214 J.C. McKendry/iStockphoto, 215l Jeff Foott/Getty Images, 215r Derek Dammann/iStockphoto, 216l Armin Rose/Dreamstime.com, 216r Bob Ainsworth/Dreamstime.com, 217 Julien Grondin/iStockphoto, 218t Anna Yu/iStockphoto, 218b Hashim Pudiyapura/Dreamstime.com.